ASTROPHYSICS
FOR
YOUNG PEOPLE
in a HURRY

ALSO BY NEIL deGRASSE TYSON

Accessory to War (with Avis Lang)

Astrophysics for People in a Hurry

StarTalk: The Book

Welcome to the Universe: An Astrophysical Tour
(with Michael A. Strauss and J. Richard Gott III)

The Inexplicable Universe
A SIX-PART VIDEO LECTURE SERIES

Space Chronicles: Facing the Ultimate Frontier (edited by Avis Lang)

The Pluto Files: The Rise and Fall of America's Favorite Planet

Death by Black Hole: And Other Cosmic Quandaries

Origins: Fourteen Billion Years of Cosmic Evolution
(with Donald Goldsmith)

My Favorite Universe
A TWELVE-PART VIDEO LECTURE SERIES

Cosmic Horizons: Astronomy at the Cutting Edge
(edited by Steven Soter and Neil deGrasse Tyson)

The Sky Is Not the Limit: Adventures of an Urban Astrophysicist

One Universe: At Home in the Cosmos
(with Charles Liu and Robert Irion)

Just Visiting This Planet

Universe Down to Earth

Merlin's Tour of the Universe

Bright exploding stars like the one
here, shining below the disk galaxy,
helped astrophysicists determine
that the universe is expanding
faster than we expected.

ASTROPHYSICS FOR YOUNG PEOPLE in a HURRY

NEIL DeGRASSE TYSON

with Gregory Mone

Norton Young Readers

An Imprint of W. W. Norton & Company
Independent Publishers Since 1923

For information about permission to reproduce selections
from this book, write to Permissions, W. W. Norton & Company, Inc.,
500 Fifth Avenue, New York, NY 10110

For information about special discounts for bulk
purchases, please contact W. W. Norton Special Sales at
specialsales@wwnorton.com or 800-233-4830

Manufacturing by Worzalla
Book design by Charles Kreloff Design
Production manager: Julia Druskin
Digital production: Joe Lops

ISBN: 978-1-324-00328-1
        978-0-393-35650-2 (pbk.)

W. W. Norton & Company, Inc., 500 Fifth Avenue, New York, N.Y. 10110
www.wwnorton.com

W. W. Norton & Company Ltd., 15 Carlisle Street, London W1D 3BS

1 2 3 4 5 6 7 8 9 0

CONTENTS

Prologue:
Walking Dogs to
See the Stars

I decided to become an astrophysicist when I was nine years old. I remember the night. The sky was full of stars. The Big and Little Dippers. The planets Jupiter and Saturn. A meteor streaked toward the horizon, and I saw what looked like a cloud moving across the sky. Yet it was not a cloud at all. I was looking out at our very own cosmic neighborhood, the Milky Way galaxy, a region of space crowded with one hundred billion stars. For nearly an hour I watched all this action with wonder.

Then the lights came back on, and I found myself sitting in the American Museum of Natural History's planetarium.

What I'd seen was a star show, but that did not limit the impact. That night, I knew what I wanted to be when I grew up. I was going to be an astrophysicist.

At the time I could barely pronounce the term correctly. But it is actually a rather simple concept. Astrophysics is the study of planets, stars, and other cosmic bodies and how they work and interact with one another.

Astrophysicists study black holes, the strange monsters that swallow up all light and matter within their reach. We watch the skies for signs of supernovas, the brilliant explosions of dying stars.

We are a curious, unusual bunch. A year, to an astrophysicist, is the time it takes for our planet to complete its annual trip around the Sun. If you attend an astrophysicist's birthday party, you're more likely to hear everyone sing:

Happy orbit of the Sun to you...

Science is always on our minds. As a joke, an actor friend of mine recently read me the classic bedtime story *Goodnight Moon*. You don't need a scientist to tell you that cows can't really jump over the Moon, as one does in the book. But an astrophysicist can figure out what she'd have to do to complete the feat. If the cow aims for where the Moon will be in three days, then leaps at about 25,000 miles per hour, she might have a chance.

I didn't know much about astrophysicists when I was nine. I merely wanted to understand what I'd seen during that planetarium show, and whether the real cosmos, the universe as a whole, was truly that fantastic. First, I began studying the sky from the rooftop of my apartment building, sneaking up with one of my friends and his handy binoculars. Later, I started a dog-walking business so I could buy my own telescope. There were large dogs, small ones, mean ones, and friendly ones. Dogs with raincoats. Dogs with hats and booties. I walked them all so I could see the stars.

In the years since, I've used steadily larger telescopes, moving from that New York rooftop to South American mountaintops. Through it all, the common thread has been my desire to understand the cosmos, and to share my passion with as many people as possible.

That includes you.

I don't expect that everyone who reads this book will instantly want to become an astrophysicist. But maybe it will spark your curiosity. If you have ever looked up at the night sky and wondered: What does it all mean? How does it all work? And what is my place in the universe? Then I encourage you to continue reading. *Astrophysics for Young People in a Hurry* will give you a basic knowledge of the major ideas and discoveries that help scientists think about the universe. If I've succeeded, you'll be able to stun your parents at the dinner table, impress your teachers, and stare up at the stars on cloudless nights with a deeper sense of both understanding and wonder.

So let's begin. We could start with two of the grandest mysteries, dark matter and dark energy, but first we should run through what I consider to be the greatest story ever told.

The story of life.

In the last century, astronomers spotted eight exploding stars in this spiral galaxy—which is why it's called the Fireworks galaxy.

ASTROPHYSICS
FOR
YOUNG PEOPLE
in a HURRY

A clear view of the night
sky opens your eyes and
mind to the wonders of
stars, interstellar dust, and
our crowded Milky Way.

1.
The Greatest Story Ever Told

I n the beginning, nearly fourteen billion years ago, the entire universe was smaller than the period that ends this sentence.

How much smaller? Imagine that period was a pizza. Now slice the pizza into a trillion pieces. Everything, including the particles that make up your body, the trees or buildings outside your window, your friend's socks, petunias, your school, our planet's towering mountains and deep oceans, the solar system, the distant galaxies— all of the space and energy and matter in the cosmos was crammed into that point.

And it was hot.

Conditions were so hot, with so much packed into such a small space, the universe could only do one thing.

Expand.

Rapidly.

Today, we call this event the big bang, and in a tiny fraction of a second (specifically, one-ten-million-trillion-trillion-trillionth of a second), the universe grew tremendously.

What do we know about this first instant in the life of our cosmos? Very little, unfortunately. Today, we have found that four basic forces control everything from the orbits of planets to the little particles that make up our bodies. But in that instant after the big bang, all these forces were rolled into one.

As the universe expanded, it cooled.

By the end of this blip of time, which is known among scientists as the Planck era, named for the German physicist Max Planck, one force wriggled free of the others. This force, gravity, holds together the stars and planets that form galaxies, keeps Earth in orbit around the Sun, and prevents ten-year-olds from dunking basketballs. Among other things. For a simple demonstration of gravity's constant pull, close this book, lift it a few inches off the nearest table, and then let go. That is gravity at work.

(If your book did not fall, please find your nearest astrophysicist and declare a cosmic emergency.)

In the first few instants of the early universe, however, there were no planets or books or ten-year-old basketball players for gravity to act upon. Gravity does its best work with large objects, and everything in the early universe was still unimaginably small.

But this was only the beginning.

The cosmos continued growing.

Next, the other three main forces of nature separated

could You Dunk on Mars?

Let's assume you could actually get to Mars, which is not an easy task, and that you had a spacesuit that allows enough freedom of movement to let you jump. The strength of gravity on a given planet or moon depends on its mass. Since Mars is less massive than Earth, gravity is a little more than 1/3 as strong. So, there's a chance you could jump high enough. But I hope, if you do manage to make it to Mars one day, that you won't waste your time playing basketball. There will be many more interesting things to see and do.

from each other.* The main job of these forces is to control the tiny particles, or chunks of matter, that fill the cosmos.

Once the four forces had all split apart, we had what we needed to build a universe.

A trillionth of a second has passed since the beginning.

* The four forces are gravity, the strong force, the weak force, and electromagnetism. We'll talk more about them later.

The universe was still unimaginably tiny, hot, and starting to become crowded with particles. At this point, the particles came in two types, called quarks—which rhymes with marks—and leptons. Quarks are quirky beasts. You'll never catch a quark all by itself; it will always be clutching others nearby. I'm sure you have at least one friend or classmate who behaves similarly. Quarks are like those kids who never want to do anything alone, not even walk to the restroom.

The force that keeps two or more quarks together actu-

The Many Names of Matter

I was warned that it would be unwise to introduce so many names and terms to young readers. So I'll resist the temptation to detail all the different types of quarks in the universe—up, down, strange, charmed. But I do think you should know of quarks and leptons. The entire visible universe is built from them. Including you. Plus, I've noticed that kids have absolutely no trouble memorizing the complex names of various dinosaurs. Sure, some dinosaurs are ferocious and terrifying, which makes them worth memorizing. But again, we're talking about the stuff that makes up the universe! Particles are fascinating, too, even if they're less ferocious. Without them, we wouldn't have had those dinosaurs in the first place.

ally grows stronger the more you separate them—as if they were attached by some sort of miniature invisible rubber band. Separate them enough, the rubber band snaps and the stored energy creates a new quark at each end, giving each one of the separated pair a new friend. Imagine if the same thing happened to those inseparable kids at your school, and they all sprouted doubles. Your teachers would undoubtedly be stumped.

The leptons, on the other hand, are loners. The force that joins quarks together has no effect on leptons, so they don't clump together in groups. The best-known lepton is the electron.

In addition to these particles, the cosmos was seething with energy, and this energy was contained in little wave-like packets or bunches of light energy called photons.

This is where things get weird.

The universe was so hot that these photons routinely converted into matter-antimatter particle pairs. And those pairs would collide, transforming into photons once again. But for mysterious reasons, one in a billion of these conversions made just a matter particle, without its antimatter friend. If not for these lone survivors, the universe would have no matter in it at all. And that's a good thing, too. Because we're all made of matter.

We do exist, and we know that as time passed, the cosmos continued to expand and cool. As it grew larger than the size of our solar system, the temperature dropped rapidly. The universe was still incredibly hot, but the temperature had fallen below a trillion degrees Kelvin.

Antimatter

All the major particles in the universe, including the quarks and leptons we just met, have antimatter twins that are their opposites in every way. Take the electron, the most popular member of the lepton family of particles. The electron has a negative charge, but its antimatter opposite, the positron, has a positive charge. We don't see antimatter around much, though, because once a particle of antimatter is created, it immediately seeks out its matter twin, and these meetings never go well. The twins destroy each other, converting into a burst of energy. (See the story about physicist George Gamow's Mr. Tompkins in chapter 3.) Today, scientists create antimatter particles in giant experiments that smash together atoms. We observe them following high-energy collisions in space. But antimatter is probably easiest to find in science fiction plots. It fuels the engines in the famed *Enterprise* of the *Star Trek* television show and movies, and appears repeatedly in comics.

How We Measure Temperature

Maybe you've learned this already, but there are several different ways to describe the temperature of a system. Here in the United States, we speak of degrees Fahrenheit. In Europe and much of the rest of the world, the standard is degrees Celsius. Astrophysicists use Kelvin, a standard in which zero is *really* zero. You can't get any colder. So, a trillion degrees Kelvin is much hotter than a trillion degrees Fahrenheit or Celsius. I have nothing against the other standards. In my daily life, I'm fine with Fahrenheit. But when I'm thinking about the universe, it's all Kelvin.

A millionth of a second has passed since the beginning.

The universe had grown from a tiny fraction of the period at the end of this sentence to the size of our solar system. That's almost three hundred billion kilometers, or more than one hundred and eighty billion miles, across.

A trillion degrees Kelvin is much, much hotter than

A Simple Recipe for Matter in the Universe

1. Start with quarks and leptons.

2. Add quarks together to form protons and neutrons.

3. Combine the protons, neutrons, and electrons (a negatively charged type of lepton) to build your first atoms.

4. Mix these atoms together to make molecules.

5. Accumulate molecules in different forms and combinations to make planets, and petunias, and people.

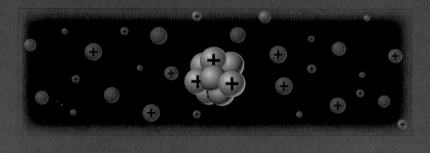

the surface of the Sun. But compared with that very first instant following the big bang, this was cool. This luke-warm universe was no longer hot enough or crowded enough to cook quarks, and so they all grabbed dance partners, creating heavier particles. These combinations of quarks soon resulted in the appearance of more familiar forms of matter like protons and neutrons.

**By now, one second of time
has passed since the beginning.**

The universe has grown to a few light-years across, about the distance from the Sun to its closest neighboring stars. The temperature has dropped to a billion degrees. This is still plenty hot—enough to cook the little electrons and their opposites, positrons. The two different particles pop into existence, annihilate each other, and disappear. But what was true for other particles becomes true for electrons: only one in a billion survives.

The rest destroy each other.

The temperature of the cosmos drops below a hundred million degrees, but it's still hotter than the surface of the Sun.

Larger particles begin to fuse with each other. The basic ingredients for the atoms that make up our visible world today—including the stars and planets, the trees or buildings outside your window, your friend's socks, my moustache—are finally coming together. Protons fuse with other protons as well as with neutrons, forming the center of the atom, called the nucleus.

The Four Fundamental Forces

Here are the four fundamental forces that control our universe:

1. Gravity, which you know.

2. The strong force holds particles together in the center of atoms.

3. The weak force causes atoms to break down and release energy. Also, it's not actually weak. It's way stronger than gravity. But it's not as powerful as the strong force.

4. The electromagnetic force binds negatively charged electrons to the positively charged protons in the center of atoms. It also binds the collections of atoms known as molecules.

But let's keep this simple: Gravity binds the big stuff, and the three other forces work on the little things.

Two minutes have now passed
since the beginning.

Normally, the electrons whipping around the universe would be attracted to the protons and nuclei. Electrons have a negative charge. The protons and nuclei have positive charges, and opposites attract. Why do they have positive and negative charges? And why, you ask, do opposites attract?

They just do.

I wish I had a better answer for you, but the universe is under no obligation to make sense to us. What I can say is that many, many years of scientific research have backed up both of these ideas.

Now, given their attraction, you'd think the protons and

what is charge?

Each of us humans has various qualities or characteristics. Maybe we're kind or charitable or unfriendly. These properties help define us. Charge is one of the basic properties of matter. Some particles, like protons, have positive charge. Others have negative charge. And still others, such as neutrons, have no charge at all. When two particles have the same charge, they are pushed apart. If they have opposite charge, such as protons and electrons, they are drawn closer together.

electrons would latch onto each other. For thousands of years, though, the universe was still too hot for them to settle down. The electrons roamed free, batting photons back and forth, something free electrons like to do.

This came to an end when the temperature of the universe fell below 3,000 degrees Kelvin (about half the temperature of the Sun's surface), and all the free electrons combined with those positively charged protons. When they joined, all those photons could now cross the universe, untouched—light that scientists can still detect today. We will talk about it more in chapter 3.

Three hundred and eighty thousand years have passed since the beginning.

The universe continued to expand like a balloon that never pops. As it grew, it cooled, and gravity started to do its work. For the first few hundred thousand years, particles were racing everywhere, like kindergartners set loose on a playground. Then gravity began pulling these pieces together into the cosmic cities called galaxies.

Nearly a hundred billion galaxies formed.

Each galaxy contained hundreds of billions of stars.

These stars acted like pressure cookers, forcing the tiny particles to bond together into larger and larger ele-

This view from a telescope shows hundreds of thousands of stars near the center of our Milky Way galaxy.

ments. The biggest stars would build up so much heat and pressure that they manufactured heavy elements like iron.

The elements inside those giant stars would be completely useless were they to remain where they formed. But these stars were unstable. They exploded, sending their insides racing across the galaxy.

Nine billion years after the beginning of the universe, in an average part of the universe in an average galaxy, an average star (the Sun) was born.

How did it form? Gravity slowly pulled together an enormous gas cloud filled with particles and heavy elements packed with added protons and neutrons. As they

what are elements?

There are 118 known elements in the universe. Each one is made from just one type of atom. The main difference between each element is the number of protons it has packed into its core. Hydrogen, which has just one proton, is the most common element in the universe. If you add a proton to a hydrogen atom, you end up with a new element, helium.

orbited around one another, gravity forced them closer and closer until they collided and fused.

Once the Sun was born, this gas cloud still had plenty of cosmic ingredients remaining. The cloud provided enough matter to make several planets, hundreds of thousands of the space rocks known as asteroids, and billions of comets. Even then, there were leftovers, and this wandering junk slammed into the other cosmic objects.

These crashes were so energetic they melted the surfaces of the rocky planets.

As the amount of stuff whipping around the solar system decreased, there were fewer of these impacts, and the planet surfaces began to cool. The one we call Earth formed in a kind of Goldilocks zone around the Sun. Goldilocks, you remember, doesn't like her porridge too hot or too cool. She wants it just right. Similarly, Earth formed at just the right distance from the Sun. Had Earth been much closer, the oceans would have evaporated. Had Earth been much farther away, the oceans would have frozen.

Looking at Earth from 700 kilometers above the surface reveals why we call ours a blue planet.

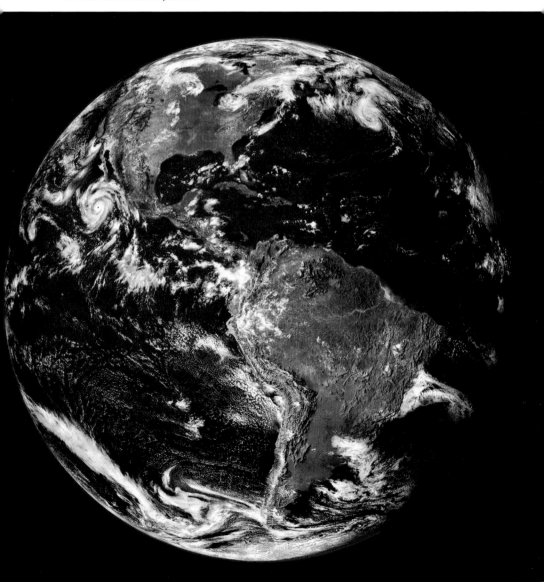

In either case, life as we know it would not have evolved.

You would not be here, reading this book.

The universe is now more than nine billion years old.

Water trapped within the rocks that made up our young, hot planet was released into the skies. As Earth cooled, this water fell as rain, gradually creating the oceans. Within these oceans, by some method we have not yet discovered, simple molecules joined together and transformed into life.

Humans are aerobic creatures. We require oxygen-rich air. The dominant players in these early oceans were simple anaerobic bacteria—microscopic life forms that don't need oxygen to survive. Thankfully, those anaerobic bacteria released oxygen, pumping the air full of the stuff we humans would eventually need to thrive. This new, oxygen-rich atmosphere allowed more and more complex forms of life to arise.

But life is fragile. Occasionally, large comets and asteroids crash into our planet and make an enormous mess.

Sixty-five million years ago, a ten-trillion-ton asteroid hit what is now the Yucatan Peninsula, in Mexico. The space rock punched a hole in the surface that was one hundred and ten miles wide and twelve miles deep. The impact, and the dust and debris it sent up into the atmosphere, obliterated most of the life on Earth, including all the famous large dinosaurs.

Extinction. The absolute end to the existence of a creature or life form.

This catastrophe allowed our mammal ancestors to thrive, rather than continue to serve as snacks for *T. rex*. One big-brained branch of these mammals, that which we call primates, evolved a species (*Homo sapiens*) with enough smarts to invent methods and tools of science—and to figure out the origin and evolution of the universe.

That's us.

What happened before the beginning?

Astrophysicists have no idea. Or, rather, our most creative answers to this question have little or no grounding in experimental science. In other words, we can't prove them. In response, some people insist that *something* must have started it all: a force greater than all others, a source from which everything issues. In the mind of these people, that something is, of course, God.

But what if the universe was always there, in a state we have yet to identify—a multiverse, for instance, that continually creates new universes?

Or what if the universe just popped into existence from nothing?

Or what if everything we know and love was just a

computer game created by a superintelligent species of aliens?

These questions usually satisfy nobody. Yet they remind us that ignorance—*not* knowing—is the natural state of mind for a research scientist. Smart young people often hate to utter the words "I don't know." But scientists have to admit what we don't know all the time. People who believe they know everything have neither looked for, nor stumbled upon, the boundary between what is known and what is unknown in the universe.

That is where I hope to take you in the following chapters.

What we do know for certain is that the universe had a beginning.

We know the universe continues to change and evolve.

And we know that every one of your body's atoms can be traced back to the big bang and the ovens in the giant stars that launched their insides across the galaxies more than five billion years ago.

We are stardust brought to life.

The universe has given us the power to figure itself out—and we have only just begun.

2.
How to communicate with Aliens

Imagine we land on another planet with a thriving alien civilization. The aliens might look nothing like us. They could have three legs. Or no legs at all. Their skin could be slimy and purple and they could be uglier than naked mole rats. Maybe they will be wonderful dancers. We just don't know. The only thing we know for certain is that their world will be following the same laws of nature as our own.

In science, we call this idea the universality of physical laws.

If you wanted to talk to the aliens, you can bet they wouldn't speak English or French or even Mandarin. Nor would you know whether shaking their hands would be considered a friendly greeting or a terrible insult. But if they are an advanced civilization, they will understand our shared physical laws. Short or tall, slimy or not, they'll know about gravity. So your best hope is to find a way to communicate using the language of science.

The scientific rules that define and shape our world are the same everywhere in the universe, from your backyard to the surface of Mars and beyond. Even the *Star Wars* movies, which take place in a galaxy far, far away, should stick to these laws, since the most distant galaxies remain part of our cosmos.

Scientists did not always know that physical laws were universal. Until the year 1666, when a gentleman named Isaac Newton wrote down the law of gravitation, a kind of recipe for how gravity works, nobody had any reason to think that the scientific rules here at home were the same as they were everywhere else in the universe. Earth had earthly things going on and the heavens—the stars and planets—had heavenly things going on.

In our own lives, rules can change from one place to the next. You might be allowed to stomp all around your house or apartment with your sneakers on. But if you go over to your friend's place, the rules might demand that you slip off your shoes at the door to avoid tracking mud everywhere. Scientists used to think the cosmos operated the same way. Newton discovered that the universe works differently.

The same laws apply everywhere.

In 1665, people were fleeing the city of London to avoid a deadly infection known as the plague. Sir Isaac Newton joined them, retreating to his country estate in Lincolnshire. Away from the city, Newton had some time on his hands, so he did a little thinking. Staring at his orchard, he began wondering what kind of force pulled ripe apples from a tree. Why did they fall straight to the ground? By 1666, this question helped him work out the laws of gravity.

The genius of Newton's work was in realizing that gravity did not merely yank apples down to the grass. He figured out that gravity also holds the Moon in orbit around Earth.

Newton's law of gravity steers planets, asteroids, and comets around the Sun.

It prevents the hundreds of billions of stars in our Milky Way galaxy from spinning off into the cosmos.

Gravity is not the only law with this kind of reach.

Sir Isaac Newton realized that gravity doesn't just pull apples from trees. It also holds the Moon in orbit around Earth.

Since Newton's day, scientists have discovered many other physical laws that operate the same way everywhere. This universality of physical laws helps scientists make fantastic discoveries. We can study distant stars and planets and assume they follow the same rules.

After Newton, nineteenth-century astronomers used this idea to determine that the Sun is made of the same elements they'd been studying on Earth, including hydrogen, carbon, oxygen, nitrogen, calcium, and iron. They even found the traces of a new element in sunlight. Being of the Sun, the new substance was given a name derived from the Greek word *helios* ("the Sun"). Helium became the first and only member of the grand collection of elements known as the Periodic Table to be discovered someplace other than Earth. Many years later, birthday parties were forever changed as kids discovered they could suck in a draft of the gas from balloons and transform their voices to a cartoonish pitch.

Okay, these laws work in the solar system, but do they operate throughout the galaxy?

Across the universe?

And were they around a million or even a few billion years ago?

Step by step, the laws were tested.

Astronomers found that nearby stars were also made of familiar building blocks like hydrogen and carbon. Later, while studying binary stars, or pairs of stars that circle each other like hesitant fighters in a boxing ring, astronomers once again discovered gravity's influence. The same universal law that pulled Newton's apples from his tree and prevents fifth-graders from dunking basketballs binds these pairs together and allows scientists to predict their movements.

When gravity pulls two powerful stars closer together, the results can be explosive, as this artist's version shows.

So the laws work here, and far away. But how do we know they've always been true? Were these universal laws operating a million years ago?

Yes. We know this because astrophysicists can see into the past.

When you stare at Mars through a telescope, you're not viewing the Red Planet as it is at that instant. The distance between Earth and Mars changes, but let's say it's one hundred and forty million miles away. That means the light has to travel one hundred and forty million miles

The light from Mars travels through space before reaching our telescopes, so we actually see the planet as it was several minutes earlier.

to reach us, a trip that takes about twelve minutes for a
light beam. Since it took twelve minutes for the light to
reach your telescope, you're actually seeing Mars as it was
twelve minutes ago.

Astrophysicists have much bigger telescopes, so we can
study objects much farther away, and the farther away we
look in space, the farther back in time we see.

I know what you're thinking: *Whoa.*

Yes, that is the appropriate response.

We talk about the distance to faraway stars and galaxies

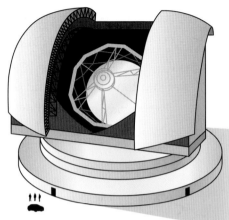

in terms of light-years, or the time it takes a beam of light to travel from that object to our telescopes. So when we study a galaxy five billion light-years away, this means it took five billion years for the light to get here.

In other words, we're seeing that galaxy as it was five billion years ago.

We literally look back in time, and we find that the most distant objects in the universe, which are billions of years old, follow the same rules we observe today. Across the cosmos, the universal laws have been hard at work since the beginning.

Of course, the universality of physical laws doesn't mean that all things that happen in the cosmos take place here on Earth. Just because the laws are the same everywhere doesn't mean everything is possible everywhere. For instance, I'd bet you've never greeted a black hole on the street.

These cosmic monsters form when gravity collapses incredibly dense stars. Gravity sucks all the matter in the star into the center, leaving a hole in space where the star once shone. The gravitational force around these black holes is so powerful that not even light can escape them. If a cosmic pothole like that really did appear on the street, you wouldn't be the only victim. The entire planet could be drawn into the vortex and disappear.

But as powerful as they are, black holes still follow the laws of nature.

Physical laws are not the only things that apply everywhere in the universe. These laws also depend on numbers called constants, which help scientists predict the effect a given law is going to have. The constant of gravitation, known as "big G," helps scientists figure out how strong gravity will be in a given situation. For instance, we can use big G to help us estimate the surface gravity on Mars.

Among all constants, though, the speed of light is the most famous. During the Apollo missions, it took astronauts about three days to fly to the Moon. If they'd traveled at light speed, the two-hundred-and-forty-thousand-mile trip would have taken a little more than a second. So why didn't they? It's impossible.

No experiment has ever revealed an object of any form reaching the speed of light.

No matter how fast we go, we will never outrun a beam of light.

Humans accomplish the seemingly impossible all the time. We also underestimate our engineers and inventors.

People once said we'd never fly. They insisted we'd never be able to travel to the Moon or split the atom. We have since accomplished all three. But in each case, no established laws of physics stood in the way.

Going to the Moon was hard, but not impossible.

The claim "We will never outrun a beam of light" is a totally different prediction. It flows from basic, time-tested physical principles. The universe might as well be posted with speed limit signs that read:

The Speed of Light: It's Not Just a Good Idea It's the Law

Aliens, no matter how advanced or intelligent, won't be able to outrace a light beam either. But they will probably be familiar with these constants. All our scientific research, measurements, and observations of the cosmos suggest that the major constants, from the big G to the speed of light, and the physical laws that use them, never change with time or location.

Maybe I seem a little too sure of myself. Scientists don't know everything. Not even close. We don't agree on everything, either. We argue as intensely as siblings. But when we do, our arguments focus on concepts and cosmic happenings we barely understand.

When a universal physical law is involved, the debate is guaranteed to be brief.

Yet not everyone grasps this idea.

A few years ago I was having a hot cocoa at a dessert shop in Pasadena, California. Ordered it with whipped cream, of course. When my cocoa arrived at the table, I saw no trace of the stuff. After I told my waiter that my cocoa had no whipped cream, he insisted I couldn't see it because it sank to the bottom.

But whipped cream has low density. It floats on all the liquids we humans drink, including hot chocolate. Wherever you are in the universe, substances with low density will float in liquids with higher density. This is a universal law.

So I offered the waiter two possible explanations: either somebody forgot to add the whipped cream to my hot cocoa or the universal laws of physics were different in his restaurant. Unconvinced, he brought over a dollop of whipped cream to demonstrate his claim. After bobbing once or twice the whipped cream rose to the top, safely afloat.

What better proof do you need of the universality of physical law?

3.
Let There Be Light

I met Superman once. This happened in the pages of a comic book, but it felt real. In this particular issue, "Star Light, Star Bright," the Man of Steel has been busy fighting off a horde of alien invaders on Mars when he takes a break. He leaves the battle to his Justice League friends and flies back to Earth, all because he wants to see a star.

That's my kind of superhero.

If you're not familiar with Superman, he has bulletproof skin, eyes that can shoot lasers, the ability to fly, and a few other impressive capabilities. More importantly, though, he's an alien. He was born on a planet called Krypton and traveled to Earth as an infant in a spacecraft. After his journey through space, he landed in a field in Kansas, met his new parents, Jonathan and Martha Kent, and got on with his life.

Here's a look at what happens after a star explodes, vomiting its insides across the galaxy in all directions.

While he was on his way to Earth, though, Krypton was destroyed. The comics and movies offer different versions of how this happened, but in "Star Light, Star Bright," Krypton's sun goes supernova. The star explodes, roasting Superman's home planet in the process.

My contribution to the issue, besides lending myself as a character, complete with my moustache and my favorite astronomy-themed vest, was figuring out where Superman's home might be located in our actual galaxy. The writers asked for my help and, after a little research,

I picked a nice neighborhood in the constellation Corvus, about twenty-seven light-years from Earth. Again, that's the distance it would take a beam of light to cover while racing across the universe for twenty-seven years.

I picked Corvus as Superman's home address because its light needs to travel for twenty-seven years before reaching us. This way, the light from its final moments didn't arrive until he was an adult.

So, in a word, far.

When Superman first travels to Earth, his ship carries him faster than the speed of light. Yes, this is impossible, as we discussed in the last chapter. But since they are actually intelligent aliens, maybe they figured out how to create

wormholes

One of Albert Einstein's big ideas was that gravity could actually change the shape of space, turning straight lines into curves. But if you stretch this idea to its extreme, then it becomes possible to bend whole sections of the universe and bring distant locations close together. Pretend our universe is reduced to a simple piece of paper. If you were to draw a picture of Earth in one corner, then add a circle representing Krypton in the opposite corner, the shortest distance between the two would be a straight line, right? Normally, yes. But if gravity were to bend this flattened universe, and you folded the paper over so that the two planets were close to touching, then the shortest distance changes. A wormhole—Einstein referred to it as a bridge—is a kind of tunnel through space that connects these distant points. We don't know if they actually exist, or if you'd be able to travel through one safely in a spaceship without every atom in your body being torn apart, but science fiction writers certainly do love them.

wormholes and travel through them. This gets you wherever you want in the universe by taking a shortcut.

Superman arrives on Earth, but when his sun explodes,
the light from that event has to travel across space at the
usual speed. While Superman is growing up on Earth,
learning about farming, memorizing his state capitals, and
discovering his powers, the light beams from that exploding star are still on their way across the cosmos.

When he becomes an adult, moves to Metropolis,
which is really just a variation of my hometown, New York
City, and transforms into the famed Man of Steel, the light
beams are still traveling.

When he falls in love with Lois Lane, those beams of
light still haven't arrived yet.

When he heads to Mars to fight off the invading aliens,
the photons are finally getting close. Since the star is
twenty-seven light-years from Earth, and his sun explodes
right after his birth, Superman is twenty-seven years old
when the light from that supernova finally reaches our
telescopes.

That's when the Man of Steel rushes to the Hayden
Planetarium to visit yours truly. In the story, the comic version of me has arranged it so that all of Earth's most powerful telescopes are aimed toward Corvus, to capture as
much light as possible—visible and invisible.

This a terribly sad moment for the big guy. He finally
sees for certain that his home planet has been toasted by
a supernova. But it's a perfect illustration of one of the
strangest things about astrophysics—or even nature itself.

We've been over this idea already, but it's worth revisiting. Light needs time to travel from its source to our telescopes. So, whenever we look at something, whenever the light from an object strikes our eyes, we are really seeing that thing as it was in the past, when the photons first started on their journey. The farther out in space we look, the longer light has to travel, and the farther back in time we see.

Looking back in time twenty-seven years, as Superman and I do in the comic book, is normal for astrophysicists. Today, our telescopes and detectors allow us to gaze billions of years into the past. We can almost see back to the very beginning of the universe. For this, we can thank a pair of scientists named Arno Penzias and Robert Wilson, who made one of the greatest astrophysical discoveries of the twentieth century by accident.

In 1964, Penzias and Wilson were working for Bell Telephone Laboratories, the research branch of AT&T (American Telephone and Telegraph), the same company that provides wireless and smartphone service today. We'll cover this in more detail in chapter 9, but the sky is filled with different kinds of light energy. Some, like the familiar colors of the rainbow, are visible. Others are invisible. But they are all waves, and one of the main differences between these forms of light is their wavelengths, or the distance from one peak in a wave to the next. AT&T had

Scientists at Bell Telephone Laboratories used this antenna to learn about the birth of the universe.

built a giant, horn-shaped antenna to send and receive radio waves.

Penzias and Wilson pointed their giant antenna at the sky, but wherever they aimed the device, it picked up another form of light, microwaves. Today, most American kitchens have microwave ovens, which cook or reheat food by flooding it with these long, invisible, low-energy waves. But why were the scientists finding all these microwaves?

Penzias and Wilson were stumped.

They searched for potential sources, both on Earth and in space. In almost every case, they could explain

where the light was coming from. But one microwave signal remained a mystery. No matter where they pointed the
antenna, the scientists found this signal. Naturally they
wondered if something was wrong with their detector. The
two scientists looked inside the antenna and found pigeons
nesting there. The antenna was also covered with a white
substance.

Pigeon poop.

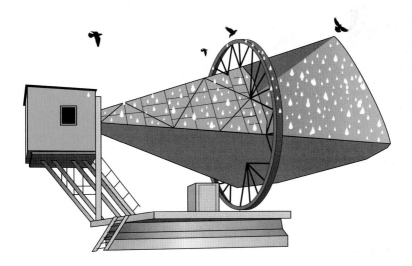

The pigeon droppings covered most of the dish. So
the mysterious microwaves could have just been a dirty
antenna. Penzias and Wilson cleaned away the substance,
encouraged the pigeons to find a new place to live, and
tested the instrument again.

The signal dropped slightly, but not completely. So it
wasn't all the pigeons' fault. Yet the scientists still did not
have an explanation for the mysterious light.

Meanwhile, a team of physicists at Princeton University, led by Robert Dicke, heard about their work. But unlike Penzias and Wilson, they knew exactly where the strange light was coming from.

Penzias and Wilson didn't have a pigeon poop problem. They had discovered light from the early universe.

After the big bang, the universe expanded rapidly.

The cosmos has many mysterious rules, as we have discussed, and one of these says that energy cannot be created or destroyed. This is known as the law of conservation of energy, and you can't break it. Really. All the energy in our universe today was around at the time of the big bang. As the cosmos grew, all that energy was stretched out over a larger and larger space. With each passing moment the universe got a little bit bigger, a little bit cooler, and a little bit dimmer.

For 380,000 years, things carried on that way.

In this early period, if your mission had been to see across the universe, you couldn't. You would need to see photons that had made this cosmic trip, but back then, photons couldn't travel very far. Have you ever tried to leave your house only to have a parent stop you at the door and remind you of an unfinished chore or some neglected homework? Such was the life of a photon. Electrons were constantly stopping them before they'd even started on their journey. Since the photons couldn't get anywhere, there was nothing to see. The universe was a glowing fog in every direction.

As the temperature dropped, however, the particles moved more and more slowly. Eventually the electrons slowed just enough to be captured by passing protons. Once electrons and protons had joined together, we had atoms.

So what does this have to do with pigeon poop?

Now that the protons were grabbing those electrons, nothing was stopping the photons anymore. They were set free to travel on uninterrupted paths across the universe.

As they raced across the cosmos, the universe continued expanding and cooling. The photons became weaker and weaker. At first, they were energetic enough to be visible—

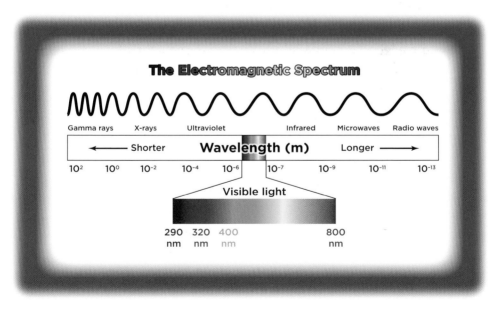

the kind of photons our eyes capture when we're staring at the printed or electronic page of a book. After traveling for millions and then billions of years, these photons cooled. They were stretched out, transforming into long, low-energy microwaves. Together, all these long-traveling photons make up what we call the "cosmic microwave background."

Don't let that somewhat fancy scientific name confuse you. And please resist the temptation to imagine a giant microwave oven floating somewhere out in space. The cosmic microwave background is the leftover light from a dazzling, sizzling early universe.

And it is the same light that Penzias and Wilson caught with their dish.

George Gamow

In addition to being an influential cosmologist, George Gamow was a successful teacher. One of his students, Vera Rubin, would make important discoveries about dark matter, the mysterious substance holding together distant galaxies. Gamow even wrote books for children. One series features a character named Mr. Tompkins who embarks on all kinds of strange scientific adventures. At one point Mr. Tompkins becomes an electron, and, like the particles in our early universe, is annihilated when he meets his antimatter twin, the positron. Tough ending.

The scientists were looking at the universe as it was nearly fourteen billion years ago.

The existence of the cosmic microwave background was predicted decades earlier by a Russian-born American physicist, George Gamow. When Dicke and his colleagues at Princeton learned of the strange signal discovered by Penzias and Wilson, they knew what it really meant. They'd been looking for evidence of the cosmic microwave background themselves. Everything fit, including that the signal came from every direction in the sky.

More than a decade later, in 1978, the discovery of the cosmic microwave background earned Penzias and Wilson the highest honor in science, the Nobel Prize.

Was It Fair?

Robert Dicke, the scientist who helped Penzias and Wilson understand what they were seeing with their telescope, did not win the award. This might seem unfair. But the Nobel Prize typically goes to a discovery. If the theorist, the person who explains what is being observed, participates in the discovery or tells the others what to look for, then he or she might share the prize. But in this case, Penzias and Wilson found the cosmic microwave background first, so they earned the award.

How do we know we're right about the cosmic microwave background?

Consider the alien point of view. Remember, light takes time to reach us from distant places in the universe. If we look out in deep space, we actually see far back in time. So if the intelligent inhabitants of a galaxy far, far away were to measure the temperature of the cosmic microwave background right before those photons start traveling to our telescopes, their result should be slightly higher than our own measurement, because they would be living in a younger, smaller, hotter universe.

You can actually test this idea.

The molecule cyanogen gets excited when exposed to microwaves. By "excited" I mean that its electrons jump to a different level as they orbit the nucleus, but if you want to picture them dancing, that's okay, too. Warmer microwaves excite cyanogen a little more than colder ones do. Astrophysicists have compared the cyanogen we see in our own Milky Way galaxy to the cyanogen in distant, younger galaxies. Since those galaxies are younger, the cyanogen is bathed in warmer microwaves, so it should be more excited. And that's exactly what we observe.

You can't make this up.

Why should any of this be interesting? Because it creates a rich picture of how the universe formed. Since Penzias and Wilson, astrophysicists have used increasingly sensitive tools to create a detailed map of the cosmic microwave background. This map is not completely smooth. It's got spots that are slightly hotter and slightly cooler than average. By studying these temperature differences, these bumps in the map, we can figure out what the early universe looked like, and where the matter started to clump together.

We can see where and when the first galaxies started to form.

The cosmic microwave background tells us that we understand how the universe behaved and expanded. But the cosmic microwave background also reveals that most of the universe is made up of stuff about which we are clueless. These two mysteries are the subject of chapters 5 and 6.

Beware, reader. Our story will soon grow dark.

4.
Between the Galaxies

The summer after finishing ninth grade, I climbed into a van with a bunch of other kids and we were driven fifty-three straight hours from New York City to the Mojave Desert of Southern California. Our destination was Camp Uraniborg, a monthlong getaway for science-minded young people named after the observatory of the Danish astronomer Tycho Brahe, pronounced "Tee-you-ko Brah," a brilliant observer with a brass nose. We'll meet him later.

I'd observed the sky before. As I said before, on clear nights I would climb up to the rooftop of our Bronx apartment building to study the stars and planets. This wasn't easy work. Often I had to recruit my little sister to help me carry up the parts of my telescope. On several occasions, our neighbors called the police, thinking a burglar was sneaking around on the rooftop.

Saturn to the Rescue

As part of my effort to prove to these police officers that I was a young astronomer, and not a criminal, I'd offer them a view of the night sky. Saturn always proved popular. It is a stunningly beautiful planet, and on those occasions, it helped prevent me from being wrongly arrested.

Really, how could you not love Saturn? Look at those rings! It's a solar system wonder like no other.

We could see stars in the city sky. A few dozen on average. Maybe a hundred.

The Mojave Desert revealed a far more crowded universe. The entire sky was filled with stars. This was like my first planetarium show, only it was real. Over the next month I recorded images of moons, planets, star systems, galaxies, and more. But I still didn't see everything. The observable universe, or the parts of the cosmos we can see, may contain a hundred billion galaxies. Bright and beautiful and packed with stars, galaxies decorate the night sky. Because they're in your face, it would be easy to believe that nothing else out there is important. But the universe contains hard-to-detect things between the galaxies. Those things may be more interesting than the galaxies themselves.

These dark stretches between the galaxies make up what we call intergalactic ("inter" means "between") space. Pretend for a moment that you were suddenly transported there. Let's ignore the fact that you would slowly freeze to death or that your blood cells would burst while you suffocated. Never mind that you would pass out and start to puff up like a kid having a massive allergic reaction.

These are ordinary dangers.

Why We Call It the Milky Way

When we study the cosmos, we tend to focus on the galaxies because they are so eye catching. Our own galaxy, the Milky Way, has a spiral shape, and is named for its spilled-milk appearance across Earth's nighttime sky. Indeed, the very word "galaxy" derives from the Greek *galaxias*, "milky."

You might also be struck by super-duper high-energy, fast-moving, charged subatomic particles called cosmic rays. We don't know where they come from or what launches them on their journey. We do know most of them are protons, and that they travel almost as fast as the speed of light. A single cosmic ray particle carries enough energy to knock a golf ball from anywhere on a putting green into a cup. NASA is so worried about what cosmic rays might do to astronauts that the agency designs its spacecraft with special shielding to block those rays.

Yes, intergalactic space is, and will forever be, where the action is.

When viewed through proper telescopes, our Milky Way galaxy appears as a thick smear across the sky. Not exactly milky, but close.

If scientists didn't have advanced telescopes, we might still declare the space between the galaxies to be empty. The bright stars and splotchy, milky galaxies dominate the night sky, and hold enough secrets to keep astrophysicists busy for centuries.

But as we discussed earlier, light comes in many forms. We are all familiar with visible light, but it can also be invisible. The X-rays that doctors and hospitals use to peer through your skin and see whether you've broken any bones after an accident are a form of light. So are the microwaves drifting in from the distant universe, offering clues to the birth of the cosmos. Even the radio waves that give us Wi-Fi are distant, low-energy cousins of the visible light that floods and colors the world all around us.

Modern detectors and probes can study these invisible forms of light. They can tell us about cosmic events and happenings that we cannot see with our eyes alone. Using these detectors, we have probed our cosmic countryside and revealed all manner of fantastic space oddities.

Allow me to introduce you to a few of my favorites.

Dwarf Galaxies

In a given area of space, there will be ten small galaxies—known as dwarf galaxies—for every large one. Our own Milky Way has dozens of nearby dwarf galaxies. While a normal, large galaxy might have hundreds of billions of stars, dwarf galaxies can have as few as a million. That might still seem impressive. But because dwarf galaxies

In the dwarf galaxy at the center of this image, stars are still forming in the bright, whitish patches.

have fewer stars, they are much, much dimmer in the sky, which makes them harder to find.

We are discovering new ones all the time.

You will find most (known) dwarf galaxies hanging out near bigger galaxies, orbiting around them like spaceships. Ultimately, the dwarfs are ripped apart, and then eaten, by the main galaxy.

The Milky Way engaged in at least one act of cannibalism in the last billion years, when it swallowed a dwarf galaxy. The shredded remains of this galaxy can be seen as a stream of stars orbiting the center of the Milky Way. These cosmic leftovers are known as the Sagittarius Dwarf system. But given that they were so rudely eaten, we should have named them Lunch.

Runaway Stars

Galaxies are grouped together into clusters, in the same
way nearby towns and cities are lumped together into
counties. But our cities and towns tend to stay put. New
York doesn't spin up the coast and crash into Boston.
Large galaxies, on the other hand, routinely collide, and
when they do, they leave behind an enormous mess.
After one of these crashes, hundreds of millions of stars,
normally held in place by gravity, escape its pull. These
stars scatter, ending up spread across the sky. Some

This massive runaway star is traveling so fast that it creates a shock
wave out in front of itself—visible here as a curved red streak.

stars reassemble to form blobs that could be called dwarf galaxies.

Other stars remain adrift. Our observations suggest that there may be as many homeless stars as there are stars within the galaxies themselves.

Exploding Runaway Stars

Some of astrophysicists' favorite cosmic events are supernovas, stars that have blown themselves to smithereens and, in the process, glow a billion times brighter for a

What could possibly be more awesome than a runaway star? An exploding runaway star! The one shown here is ejecting gas and dust.

period of several weeks. With advanced telescopes, we can see supernovas across the universe. Most of them happen within galaxies, but scientists have found more than a dozen supernovas that exploded far away from any galactic neighborhood. Normally, for every star that goes supernova, a hundred thousand to a million nearby stars do not. So those dozen exploding stars out in the middle of nowhere may be clues to the existence of many more stars that we cannot see.

Some of those undiscovered, unexploded stars could be similar to our own Sun.

Planets could be orbiting those stars, and maybe even supporting intelligent life.

Million-Degree Gas

Matter, the stuff from which everything in the universe is built, generally comes in three forms or phases: solid, liquid, and gas. The easiest example is water, which is ice in its solid form, clear and drinkable in its liquid state, and transforms into vapor when it becomes a gas.

Some telescopes have revealed a gas that stretches across the spaces between galaxies, glowing at tens of millions of degrees. Even though it's not clumped together, this gas is still made of matter. It's also very, very hot.

When galaxies move through this superheated gas, it strips them of all their excess matter, like the lunchroom bully who grabs the chocolate chip cookie off your tray as you walk past. The superheated gas doesn't just ruin a galaxy's day, though. By removing all that extra matter, it prevents the galaxy from making new stars.

Faint Blue Galaxies

Outside the major clusters, there is a population of galaxies that thrived long ago. As we already discussed, looking out into the cosmos is like looking back in time. The travel time for light to reach us from distant galaxies can be millions or even billions of years.

When the universe was one-half of its current age, a very blue and very faint type of midsized galaxy dominated. We see them today. They are difficult to detect not only because they are far away but because they contained so few bright stars. These faint blue galaxies no longer exist. What happened to them is a cosmic mystery. Did all their stars burn out? Have they become invisible corpses spread across the universe? Did they change into the dwarf galaxies we see today? Or were they all eaten by larger galaxies?

Did all of them become lunch?

We don't know.

Vacuum Energy

Even empty space isn't really empty. We refer to these regions as vacuums—not the noisy household cleaning machines, but areas that contain no matter or energy at all. But in these supposedly empty regions, oceans of virtual particles are constantly popping in and out of existence. When they meet, they often destroy each other and release energy. These miniature collisions create what scientists call "vacuum energy"—an outward pressure that acts against gravity and may help drive the expansion of the universe.

Why We Hate Vacuums

There is an old saying in science that nature abhors, or hates, a vacuum. It is an established fact that children detest vacuums, too. So do dogs. But these truths refer to the cleaning appliance. How would you feel about the intergalactic version of the vacuum? I suspect you wouldn't be overly fond of it, either. As detailed earlier in the chapter, it wouldn't be a very nice place to hang out. Why nature hates vacuums, and insists on filling them with strange activity, we do not know. It just does.

With all this stuff between the big galaxies, some of it might block our view of what lies beyond. This could be a problem for the most distant objects in the universe, such as quasars, pronounced *kway-zarz*. Quasars are the incredibly bright centers of galaxies—in scientific terms,

The quasar in this artist's illustration is shining a beam of energy across the cosmos.

superluminous galaxy cores. Their light has typically been traveling for billions of years before reaching our telescopes.

Quasar light changes slightly as it races through gas clouds and other space junk, and astrophysicists can study this light to reveal what happened along that billion-plus-year journey. For example, we can tell if the quasar light passed through multiple gas clouds. Every known quasar, no matter where on the sky it's found, shows features from dozens of different clouds scattered across time and space.

So even though these clouds aren't visible, we know they are there.

The combination of hungry galaxies, runaway stars, and superheated gas clouds certainly makes intergalactic space an interesting place. Add in those super-duper high-energy charged particles and the mysterious vacuum energy, and one could argue that all the fun in the universe happens between the galaxies rather than within them.

But I wouldn't suggest vacationing there. Your trip might at first be interesting, but it would end very, very badly.

5.
Dark Matter

Years ago, when my daughter was a toddler, she performed a fascinating experiment from her booster seat. As I watched, she carefully dropped nearly two dozen overcooked peas from her dinner plate. She let them go one at a time, and not a single pea disobeyed the universal law of gravity. Each one fell directly to the floor.

Gravity is a marvelous force, but a troubling one.

Newton and Einstein explained how gravity affects the matter in the cosmos. Overcooked peas, ripe apples, people, planets, giant stars—their ideas apply to all the matter that we can see, touch, feel, smell, and occasionally taste. And according to Newton and Einstein, most of the matter in the universe appears to be missing. I don't mean "missing" in the sense of a lost sock.

By watching certain stars and galaxies, astrophysicists can measure the power of gravity in distant parts of the cosmos. Typically, if gravity is strong, we see a large object or objects nearby. The effect around a giant star or a black hole will be enormous, for example. The gravity around a tiny space rock drifting through the cosmos? Not so much.

For years, astrophysicists have been tracking incredibly powerful gravitational fields without enough visible mass to create that power. Something has to be there, generating all that gravity. But we don't see the stuff. Whatever is there doesn't interact with "our" matter or energy. We've now been waiting nearly a century for someone to tell us why most of the gravity we've measured in the universe—about eighty-five percent of it—is tied to some kind of material we can't detect.

We are essentially clueless.

This is a major scientific riddle, and we find ourselves no closer to an answer today than when this "missing mass" problem was first uncovered in 1937. At the time, the Swiss-American astrophysicist Fritz Zwicky was study-ing the movement of galaxies within a huge region called the Coma cluster. This cosmic neighborhood lies very far from Earth. A beam of light leaving the Coma cluster has to speed across the universe for 300 million years to reach our telescopes.

The Coma cluster appears delightfully crowded from a distance. A thousand galaxies orbit around its center, moving in all directions like bees swarming in a beehive.

Astrophysicist Fritz Zwicky first found evidence of the mysterious dark matter in this group of galaxies known as the Coma cluster.

Gravity holds the cluster together, preventing anything inside from drifting away. Zwicky measured the strength of this gravitational field by watching a few dozen of the galaxies inside.

But something wasn't right.

There was just too much gravity. So he added up the mass of all the galaxies inside. Even though Coma ranks among the largest and most massive clusters in the universe, the sum total was not enough to crank out the kind of gravity that would hold all these galaxies in place.

Something else was there.

Something he could not see.

After Zwicky, astrophysicists have discovered other galaxy clusters with the same problem. This "missing mass" remains the longest-standing unsolved mystery in astrophysics.

Today, we've settled on a term for the stuff: "dark matter."

As a kid, I lived in one of two matching apartment houses. My close friend, a classmate in elementary school, lived in the other building. Thanks to him, I learned how to play chess and poker and the board games Risk and Monopoly. More importantly, he taught me how to really use binoculars, to point them at the Moon and the stars. As I switched from binoculars to telescopes and moved from the rooftop of my building to the clear views from the desert or the open sea, I fell in love with all the amazing sights scattered across the night sky.

Yet astrophysics isn't just about what we see. It also deals with what we don't see.

Fritz Zwicky found evidence for matter he could not see within clusters or groups of galaxies. Years later, in 1976, Vera Rubin, an astrophysicist at the Carnegie Institution for Science in Washington, discovered missing mass hiding within the galaxies themselves. She was studying spiral galaxies: flat, disk-shaped collections of stars with a bright bulge in the center and several star-packed arms twisting outward. Rubin tracked how fast the stars race

Now you understand why we call them spiral galaxies, right? This one may contain a trillion stars.

around the spiral galaxy centers. At first, she found what she expected. The stars farther from the center, held tight by gravity, moved at greater speeds than stars close in.

Yet Rubin also watched the areas beyond this disk. A few bright stars and lonely gas clouds lingered out there. Since there was little visible matter between these objects and the edges of the disk, nothing was holding them tight to the rest of the rotating galaxy. Their speed should have been falling with increasing distance out there in Nowheresville. But for some reason, their speeds in fact remained high.

Rubin correctly reasoned that a form of dark matter must lie in these far-out regions, holding onto those distant objects, hiding well beyond the visible edge of each spiral galaxy. Thanks to Rubin's work, we now call these mysterious zones "dark matter haloes."

This halo problem exists under our noses, right here in the Milky Way. From galaxy to galaxy and cluster to cluster, the difference between the combined mass of the stuff we see and the amount of mass that should be there based on gravity's strength is enormous. Cosmic dark matter has about six times the total gravity of all the visible matter. Or, to put it another way, there is six times as much dark matter as normal matter.

Studying dark matter haloes like this one allowed astrophysicist Vera Rubin to find more evidence of missing mass in the cosmos.

Dark Matter Detective

As a kid, Vera Rubin watched the stars from her bedroom window, then built her first telescope out of a cardboard tube. She caught the bug early. After college, she applied to Princeton University to earn an advanced degree in astrophysics, but the school told her that the program did not accept women. That didn't stop Vera Rubin. She went on to earn her degree from another university and use her studies of spiral galaxies to prove that dark matter really does exist. Many people believe Rubin should have been awarded the Nobel Prize for her work. After all, the greatest award in science goes to discoveries, and what could be more worthy than the discovery of dark matter, the mysterious substance that glues together galaxies?

So what is this dark matter?

We know it cannot be made of ordinary matter like protons, neutrons, and the rest. We've also ruled out black holes and other cosmic oddities. Could the dark matter just be asteroids or comets? Planets wandering through space, untied to a solar system? They all have mass, but none of them produce any light of their own. They would appear dark to our detectors. In that sense, they fit. But there would not be enough of them, so we have to rule out wandering planets.

We also know that dark matter can't be made of the same particles as planets or humans or hamburgers because it doesn't seem to follow the same rules. The forces that bind the particles in our world together don't apply to dark matter. The only rule dark matter seems to follow is gravity.

Maybe there's nothing the matter with the matter, and it's the gravity we don't understand. Maybe Newton was wrong. Einstein, too. Maybe you, reader, will eventually discover, while cruising past an apple orchard in your self-driving robotic car, how gravity really works. In the meantime, we have to work with the facts we have now. And as best we can figure, dark matter isn't just matter that happens to be dark.

Instead, it's something else altogether.

Don't worry. You're not going to hit your head on a clump of dark matter while tiptoeing to the bathroom at night. You won't trip over a pile of it on your way from one class to the next in the crowded halls of your middle school, although you are more than welcome to use that as an excuse should one of your less scientifically minded classmates mock your accidental stumble. Dark matter lives in galaxies and galaxy clusters. For the smallest objects, such as moons and planets, we see no effect. The gravity on Earth can be explained entirely by the stuff that's under our feet. Down here, at least, Newton got it right.

So what is dark matter made of? What do we know about it? Normal matter clumps together into molecules and objects of all sizes, from tiny grains of sand to giant space rocks. Dark matter does not. If it did, we would find chunks of dark matter dotting the universe.

We'd have dark matter comets.

Dark matter planets.

Dark matter galaxies.

As far as we can tell, though, that's not the way things are. What we know is that the matter we have come to love in the universe—the stuff of stars, planets, and life—is only a light frosting on a much larger, darker cosmic cake.

We don't know what it is. But we do know that we need dark matter. We always have.

During the first half million years after the big bang, a mere eyeblink in the fourteen-billion-year sweep of cosmic history, matter in the universe had already begun to come together into loose blobs. These blobs would become clusters and superclusters of galaxies. But the cosmos would also double in size during its next half million years, and continue growing after that. During this growth period, two effects were competing with each other.

Gravity was working to bring everything together.

The expanding universe was working to spread everything out.

The gravity from ordinary matter could not win this battle by itself. We needed the added strength of the gravity from dark matter. Without it, we would be living in a universe with no structures.

No clusters.

No galaxies.

No stars.

No planets.

No people.

Without dark matter, we would not be here at all.

So dark matter is our frenemy. We have no clue what it is, and in that sense, it's kind of annoying. But we desperately need it. Scientists are generally uncomfortable whenever we must rely on ideas we don't understand, but we'll do it if we have to. And dark matter is not the first time we scientists have had to depend on something mysterious.

In the nineteenth century, for example, scientists measured the energy output of our Sun and showed its effect on our seasons and climate. They knew the Sun warmed us and provided some of the energy needed for life. But they had no idea how the Sun actually worked until a woman named Margaret Burbidge and her colleagues figured it out. Before Burbidge, the Sun was just as mysterious to scientists as

Why the Sun Shines

Stars like our Sun began as giant gas clouds. Gravity collapses these clouds, shrinking them smaller and smaller, and making them hotter and hotter. Some gas clouds will stop collapsing and settle as a giant, glowing mass. But others, like the one that formed our Sun, are so large that they trigger a process called thermonuclear fusion. Hydrogen molecules in the core slam into each other and combine—or fuse—and then release energy. The energy from all these little collisions pushes out against gravity, preventing the cloud from collapsing further, and provides enough energy to let the Sun shine.

dark matter. Some scientists proposed that it was really a burning lump of coal.

Dark matter is a strange idea, but it is grounded in facts. We assume it is there because of the work of Vera Rubin and Fritz Zwicky and what we still observe today. Dark matter is just as real as the distant planets astronomers have discovered in recent years. Scientists have never seen or touched or felt these exoplanets, planets that exist outside our solar system. But science is not just about seeing. It's about measuring unseen effects, too, preferably with an instrument that's more powerful and sensitive than your eyes. We know these exoplanets are real because we use our amazing instruments to study the stars they orbit. In examining those stars, we uncover solid clues of the planets' existence.

The worst that can happen is we discover that dark matter does not consist of matter at all, but of something else. Could we be seeing the effects of forces from another dimension?* Are we feeling the ordinary gravity of ordinary matter that exists in a phantom universe next to ours? If so, this could be just one of an infinite assortment of universes in a larger multiverse. There could be infinite versions of Earth. An unlimited number of versions of you.

Sounds unbelievable. But is it any more crazy than the first suggestions that Earth orbits the Sun? Back then, everyone thought Earth was the center of the universe. They thought the sky was basically a big dome. Now we know better. We know the Sun is one of a hundred billion stars in the Milky Way. And we know that the Milky Way is one of a hundred billion galaxies in the universe. Our home planet isn't as special as we once thought. We were wrong about Earth, so maybe we're wrong about dark matter, too.

Some scientists suspect that dark matter is made of a ghostly group of particles we have not yet discovered.

---

* Is that where all our lost socks have gone, too?

They're using giant machines called particle accelerators to try to make bits of dark matter here on Earth. Other groups have designed laboratories deep underground. If dark matter particles happen to wander through space, and a few coast into Earth, these underground labs should be able to detect them. Again, this probably sounds unbelievable. But scientists once accomplished a similar feat with a ghostly little particle called the neutrino.

In the 1930s, as scientists were trying to understand

Giant underground detectors like this one, which is part of the world's largest atom smasher, are helping scientists study the mystery of dark matter.

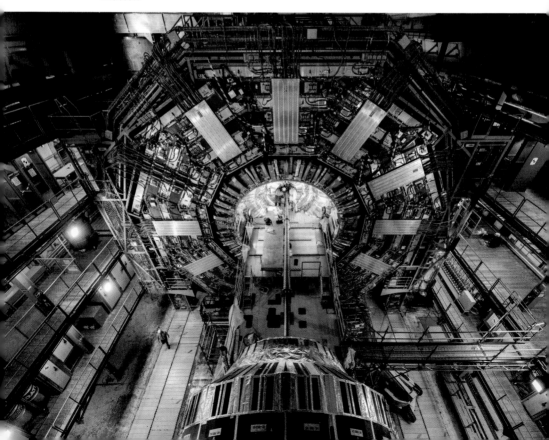

the atom, a few of the leading thinkers began to float the idea of a tiny particle that had little or no mass. They had no direct evidence of the particle at first. But certain atoms were releasing energy in an unknown way, and a few scientists suggested that these unknown particles were the culprits, carrying that energy away from the atom. Although they had no direct evidence of them, the scientists predicted the existence of neutrinos, particles that barely interact with matter. Then, a few decades later, another group of scientists discovered proof that these particles are real. Neutrinos have been tracked and counted in other experiments since then. Every second, a hundred billion neutrinos from the Sun pass through each thumbnail-sized patch of your body. And they do nothing.

What started out as a scientific hunch, a way of explaining something that didn't make sense, turned out to be real. Maybe we will find a way to detect dark matter, as we did with the neutrino. Or maybe, more amazingly, we will discover that dark matter particles are something entirely different, and that they make use of some new, undiscovered force or forces.

For now, we must remain content to carry dark matter along as a strange, invisible friend, using it to explain the universe's strange behavior. This alone would provide more than enough work for curious astrophysicists. But dark matter is not the only grand unsolved cosmic mystery. We have another fascinating puzzle to solve.

6.
Dark Energy

When I was a kid, I was fascinated by a cartoon character named Mighty Mouse. Sure, he was a rodent, but he was always saving the day, and he had this fantastic, operatic voice. The little guy could sing. Plus, he was barrel chested and incredibly strong, and he could fly.

As a curious young person, I couldn't help wondering exactly how Mighty Mouse was capable of flight. He didn't have wings. He didn't have propellers or jet engines hiding in his belt. But he did have a cape. Superman, the other famous flying hero of the day, also wore a cape. Was that the secret? Did the power of flight really just lie in your choice of outfit?

Soon I developed a theory: Capes give humans and mice the ability to fly.

Although I wasn't a scientist yet, I was starting to think like one. Science doesn't thrive on theories alone. Theories need to be tested. So I needed to set up an experiment to test my idea. I found a cape for myself, tied it around my neck, and jumped as far as I could.

I measured the distance of this cape-assisted jump.

Then I removed the cape, jumped again, and measured that distance.

There was no difference.

I didn't jump any farther with the cape. I definitely didn't fly. But I did learn a valuable lesson: In science, a theory should match the evidence collected in experiments. Otherwise, it needs to be adjusted or tossed into the garbage bin of ideas. My guess that capes allow mice and humans to fly did not match my jumping experiment, so I had to abandon my theory and move on with my life, learning to fly like the rest of humanity, in large machines called airplanes.

But sometimes even the wildest theories survive experimental tests. Albert Einstein hardly ever set foot in the laboratory. He was a pure theorist—a scientist who develops ideas about the way nature works. He perfected what's called a "thought experiment," in which you try to solve mysteries by using your imagination.

When he was sixteen years old, for example, Einstein wondered what it would be like if he were to race alongside a beam of light. This is impossible, of course. We've already discussed the cosmic speed limit. But merely thinking about this strange idea kept Einstein busy for years, and eventually led to one of his biggest breakthroughs.

Theorists like Einstein develop models of how the

universe works. Using these models, they can make predictions. If the model is broken, then the observers—the scientists who use advanced instruments to study nature—will uncover a mismatch between the prediction and the evidence. The "model" of flight I developed as a kid insisted that capes allowed humans and mice to float through the air. Then I tested the model—without the need for advanced instruments—and discovered a mismatch between my theory and the evidence. I was disappointed, but scientists are generally pretty excited when they find one of these errors in another researcher's model. We all like finding mistakes in someone else's homework.

Einstein developed one of the most powerful and far-reaching theoretical models ever, his general theory of relativity.* This model details how everything in the universe moves under the influence of gravity and how gravity shapes space itself. The general theory makes predictions that scientists are still testing today.

When black holes collide, Einstein's model predicts that they should release energy in the form of gravity waves that travel across the universe. Instead of moving through water, like the waves at a surfing beach, these cause ripples in space itself. And sure enough, scientists have caught waves from these ancient, far-off black hole collisions as they washed over Earth, proving Einstein correct.

Every few years, lab scientists come up with better experiments to test Einstein's theory. And every time, they

---

* You can call it GR. You're in the club.

show that he was right. Einstein wasn't just the smartest kid in his class. He was one of the smartest people ever.

But even he could make a mistake.

In his day, people desperately wanted to prove Einstein wrong. His work challenged Newton's ideas and some in the scientific community weren't too excited about that. A group of them joined together to publish a 1931 book titled *One Hundred Authors against Einstein*. When he learned of the book, he responded that if he were wrong, then only one author would have been enough.

General relativity was radically different from all previous thinking about gravity. According to general relativity, massive objects actually warp the space around them, causing distortions or dimples in the fabric of space and time.

A small mass like an apple has very little effect. Something large, like a planet or a star, distorts space so much that straight lines bend. One of my former teachers, the twentieth-century American theoretical physicist John Archibald Wheeler, said, "Matter tells space how to curve; space tells matter how to move."

This new version of gravity, as defined by Einstein, doesn't simply affect matter. Since gravity curves space itself, even light has to bend to gravity's power, following warped paths around massive objects instead of straight lines. Einstein's model described two kinds of gravity. One is the familiar kind: the attraction between Earth and a ball thrown into the air, or between the Sun and the planets. But general relativity also predicted another effect—a mysterious, antigravity pressure.

Today, we know that our universe is expanding. Our galaxies are spreading farther and farther apart. Back then, the idea that our universe would be doing anything at all other than simply existing was beyond anyone's imagination. Even Einstein figured the universe had to be stable, neither growing nor shrinking. But his model of the universe hinted that the universe should be either expanding or contracting. He guessed this had to be wrong. So he added a term he called the cosmological constant.

The sole job of the cosmological constant was to work against gravity in Einstein's model. If gravity was trying to pull the whole universe into one giant mass, the cosmological constant was pushing it apart.

There was just one problem.

Nobody had ever observed such a force in nature.

In a way, Einstein cheated.

Thirteen years after Einstein introduced his theory, the American astrophysicist Edwin P. Hubble discovered that the universe is not stable. Hubble had been studying distant galaxies. According to his work, these galaxies were not sitting in place. They were moving away from us! Not only that: Hubble had assembled convincing evidence that the more distant a galaxy, the faster it races away from the Milky Way.

In other words, the universe is expanding.

When he learned of the work, Einstein was embarrassed. He should have predicted it himself. He threw out the cosmological constant entirely, calling it his life's "greatest blunder." But that wasn't the end of the story. Off and on over the decades, theorists would revive the cosmological constant. They'd ask what their ideas would look like in a universe that really did have this mysterious antigravity force.

In 1998, science pulled Einstein's greatest blunder out of its grave one last time.

Early that year, two competing teams of astrophysicists made remarkable announcements. Both groups had been watching the exploding stars known as supernovas. Astronomers knew how they should behave, how bright they should glow, and how far away they were supposed to be.

But this group of supernovas was different.

They were dimmer than expected.

Two explanations were possible. Either those particular supernovas were different from all the other exploding stars that astrophysicists had studied in the past, or they were much farther away than scientists had predicted. And if they were farther away than we'd expected, then something was wrong with our models of the universe.

Hubble's work revealed that the universe was expanding, but these supernovas suggested that it was growing faster than we'd expected. And there was no easy way to make sense of this extra expansion without Einstein's blunder, the cosmological constant. When astrophysicists dusted it off and put it back into Einstein's general relativity, their observations of the universe matched his predictions.

Those supernovas were right where they were supposed to be.

This exploding star, Supernova 1987A, is pretty much a celebrity in astrophysics circles. Stars like this helped us realize that the universe is expanding.

Are Scientists Competitive?

Yes! Very much so. We're just as competitive as athletes or chess champions. Generally, in science, you don't want to get scooped. When Charles Darwin learned that another scientist, Alfred Russel Wallace, was developing some ideas that were similar to his own, he hurried to publish what would become known as his theory of evolution. He didn't want Wallace to get the credit first. This kind of thing is true for any science, but in my opinion, the universe is big enough for us all. There's plenty of research room.

The two groups of astrophysicists studying those supernovas were both awarded the Nobel Prize for their work. In the world of science, that's the equivalent of a tie.

So Einstein was correct after all.

Even when he thought he was wrong, he was right.

The discovery of these speeding supernovas was the first direct evidence that a strange new force was at work throughout the universe, fighting gravity. The cosmological constant was real, and it needed a better name. Today we call it "dark energy."

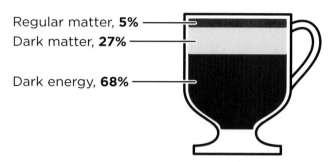

Regular matter, **5%**
Dark matter, **27%**

Dark energy, **68%**

The Universe as Hot Cocoa: A cup of hot cocoa with whipped cream and cinnamon on top. The cocoa takes up 68%, the whipped cream 27%, and the cinnamon 5%.

The most accurate measurements to date reveal dark energy as the most prominent thing in town. The universe is built from a combination of matter and energy. When we add up all the mass-energy in the universe, dark energy is currently responsible for 68 percent. Dark matter makes up 27 percent. Regular matter represents just 5 percent of the universe.

The ordinary stuff we see and feel and smell is just a sliver of the cosmos.

So what is this mystery force? Nobody knows. The closest anybody has come is to guess that dark energy is created from the vacuum of space. In chapter 4, we discussed not just the dangers of intergalactic space, but all the action happening in these seemingly empty cosmic deserts. Particles and their opposites pop into existence and destroy each other. Each pair creates a little bit of outward pressure in the process. Maybe if you were to add up all those little nudges happening all across the universe, you'd end up with enough force to power dark energy.

This is a reasonable idea. Unfortunately, when you estimate the total of this "vacuum pressure," the result is stupidly large. Much larger than our estimates of the total value of dark energy. Not counting my Mighty Mouse experiment, it would be the biggest mismatch between theory and observation in the history of science. So "vacuum pressure" can't be the source of dark energy's power.

Yes, we're clueless.

But not completely. Dark energy still arises from one of

Why It's Thrilling to Be Clueless

By this point you may have noticed that I've used this term "clueless" more than once. People often think of scientists as arrogant and always sure of themselves. But we love it when the universe stumps us. We love being clueless. It's completely exciting. It's what gets us to run to work every day. As a scientist, you learn to embrace ignorance, or not knowing. If you know all the answers, you've got nothing to work on, and you might as well just go home.

the best models of the universe we have ever developed: Einstein's general relativity. It's the cosmological constant. Whatever dark energy turns out to be, we already know how to measure it. We know how to predict its effects on the past, present, and future of the cosmos.

And the hunt is on. Now that we know dark energy is real, teams of astrophysicists are racing to find its secrets. Maybe they will succeed. Or maybe we need an alternative to general relativity. There could be some theory of dark energy that awaits discovery by a clever person yet to be born. Or maybe that future genius is reading this very book right now.

7.
My Favorite Elements

I n middle school, I asked my teacher what I thought
was a simple question about the Periodic Table of
Chemical Elements. You'll find a poster of the Periodic Table on the wall of the average science class-
room. At first glance, you could easily mistake it for a very
confusing board game. But it's not a game. The Periodic
Table tells us about all 118 elements, or types of atoms, in
the universe.

Anyway, I asked my teacher where these elements
came from.

Earth's crust, he replied.

I'll grant him that. It's surely where the school supply lab got them. But that answer wasn't enough for me.
I wanted to know how the elements ended up in Earth's

Periodic Table of the Elements

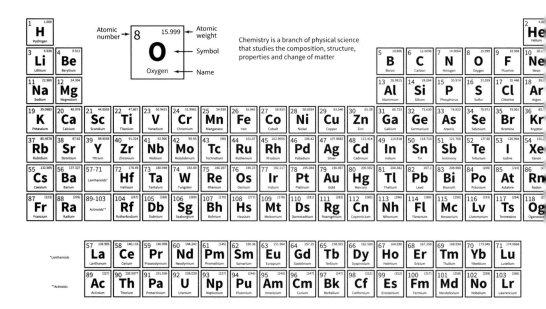

crust. Yes, I was *that* kid,* and I figured the answer must be astronomical. The elements must have originated in space. But do you actually need to know the history of the universe to answer the question?

Yes, you do.

Normal matter is made of protons, neutrons, and electrons. The protons and neutrons bunch together into something called a nucleus. The electrons, meanwhile, orbit around the outside of the nucleus. Add them together and you get what we call an atom. An element is one or more

---

* I still am.

of the same type of atom, with the same number and type of particles, and the simplest one of all is hydrogen. All it has is a single proton and a single electron. One or more of these hydrogen atoms added together is considered a hydrogen element.

Hydrogen is one of only three of the naturally occurring elements—the ones we don't make in a lab or in an experiment—that were manufactured in the big bang. The rest were forged in the high-temperature hearts and explosive remains of exploding stars. As a kind of guide to these elements, the Periodic Table is a seriously important piece of science. Yet every now and then, even a scientist can't help thinking of it as a zoo of incredibly odd, one-of-a-kind animals conceived by Dr. Seuss. These elements, after all, are unbelievably strange.

There's sodium, a poisonous metal that you can cut with a butter knife. Elsewhere on the chart you'll find chlorine, a smelly, deadly gas. The Periodic Table tells you that these two dangerous elements can be combined into one molecule. Sounds like a terrible idea. But when you add them together you make sodium chloride, better known as table salt.

Or how about hydrogen and oxygen? The first is an explosive gas. The other helps materials burn. Add oxygen to a fire and it rages. Yet the Periodic Table tells us they can pair together. When you combine hydrogen and oxygen, you make liquid water, which puts out fires.

The Periodic Table is filled with wonders. We could go

through each element and review its many strange and fantastic qualities. But as you've probably realized by now, I prefer to focus on the stars. So allow me to offer a tour of the Periodic Table as viewed through the lens of an astrophysicist.

The Most Popular Element in the Universe

The lightest and simplest element, hydrogen was made entirely during the big bang. Out of the 94 elements found in nature, hydrogen dominates. Two out of every three atoms in the human body have hydrogen in them. Nine out of every ten atoms in the entire universe are hydrogen. Every second of every day, 4.5 billion tons of fast-moving hydrogen particles slam together within the fiery hot core of the Sun. These collisions provide the energy that helps the Sun shine.

Hydrogen

The Vice President

You might recognize helium from its role in birthday parties. As a gas, helium floats nearly as well as hydrogen. But hydrogen, as I mentioned earlier, is tremendously explosive. Balloons filled with hydrogen would be a very dangerous addition to a kindergartner's birthday party. If one happened to float into a birthday candle, there would be no one left to open the presents. So we fill our balloons with helium, then suck in the strange air, speak a few lines, and sound like Mickey Mouse.

Helium is also the second simplest and second most

common element in the universe. Like hydrogen, helium was formed during the big bang. But stars make helium, too. There isn't nearly as much of it around as hydrogen, but there's still four times more of it than all other elements in the universe combined.

The Unlucky Leftover

With three protons, lithium is the third simplest element in the universe. Like hydrogen and helium, lithium was made in the big bang, and it also helps scientists test that theory. According to the big bang model, no more than one out of every one hundred atoms in any region of the universe should be lithium. No one has yet found a galaxy with more than this upper limit. This match between our predictions and what we see through our telescopes adds to the proof that the universe really did begin with a bang.

Lithium

The Life-Giving Elements

The element carbon can be found just about everywhere. Carbon is made inside stars, churned up to their surfaces, and spat out into the galaxy. You can make more molecules out of carbon than out of just about any other element. It's one of the major ingredients of life as we know it—from microscopic plants and bugs to majestic elephants and human pop stars. Selena Gomez is a carbon-based life form.

Carbon

But what about life as we don't know it? What if there

are alien life forms out there in the cosmos that are built from something other than carbon and oxygen? How about life based on the element silicon? Science fiction writers love to create stories about alien, silicon-based life forms. Exobiologists, scientists who spend their time trying to understand what life on other planets might look like, have considered this possibility, too. In the end, though, we expect most life forms will be made of carbon because there's so much more of it in the universe than silicon.

The Heavies

Aluminum occupies a large portion of Earth's crust, the thick shell that surrounds our planet's fiery center. The ancients didn't know about aluminum. Personally, I'm fond of this element because polished aluminum can

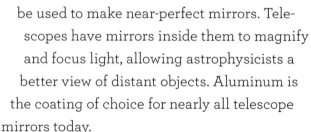

Titanium

be used to make near-perfect mirrors. Telescopes have mirrors inside them to magnify and focus light, allowing astrophysicists a better view of distant objects. Aluminum is the coating of choice for nearly all telescope mirrors today.

Another heavy element, titanium, gets its name from the powerful Greek gods, the Titans. Titanium is more than twice as strong as aluminum, and is used in military aircraft, prosthetics such as artificial legs or arms, and the shafts of lacrosse sticks. This element is also a good friend of the astrophysicist.

In most places in the cosmos, oxygen outnumbers carbon. Neither molecule likes being alone, so the carbon atoms latch onto free oxygen atoms. After all the carbon has found an oxygen atom or two, there's still some oxygen left over to bond with other elements. When oxygen bonds with titanium, the result is titanium oxide. Astrophysicists have detected traces of titanium oxide in certain stars. Recently, one group of scientists discovered a new planet surrounded by titanium oxide. We even paint parts of our telescopes with a white paint that contains titanium oxide because it helps sharpen the light from stars and other cosmic objects.

The Star Killer

Iron is not the most common element in the universe, but it might be the most important. Inside massive stars, tiny elements are constantly colliding and combining. Hydrogen atoms smash into each other to make helium. Then helium, carbon, oxygen, and others fuse. Eventually, the atoms inside are large enough to form iron, which has twenty-six protons and at least as many neutrons in its nucleus. Compared to hydrogen, with just one of each, that's enormous.

Iron

The protons and neutrons inside the iron atom are the least energetic of any element. Yet this translates into something quite simple and exciting. Because they're duds, they absorb energy. Normally, if you split an atom apart, it would release energy. The same happens if you jam two atoms together to make a new one.

But iron isn't like the other kids.

If you split iron atoms, they will absorb energy.

If you combine them, they will also absorb energy.

Stars are in the business of making energy. Our Sun, for example, is an energy factory, filling the solar system with powerful photons. But as high-mass stars start to make iron in their cores, they are nearing death. More iron means less energy. Without a source of energy, the star collapses under its own weight and explodes, outshining a billion suns for more than a week. Thanks to iron, the elements cooked in its core travel across the cosmos, providing the seeds for more stars and planets.

The Dinosaur Destroyer

Iridium ranks as the third heaviest element in the Periodic Table. This element is rare on Earth's surface, but there is a thin and widespread layer of it that offers evidence about our planet's past. Sixty-five million years ago, an asteroid the size of Mount Everest collided with Earth, vaporizing on impact, and eventually killing every land creature larger than a carry-on suitcase. So, whatever might have been your favorite theory for offing the dinosaurs, a giant killer asteroid from outer space should be at the top of your list.

Iridium

Though rare on Earth's surface, iridium is common in large metallic asteroids. When that giant space rock obliterated itself upon colliding with Earth, the iridium inside burst up and out in a giant cloud. The explosion scattered iridium atoms across the planet. Today, when scientists dig down below the ground and study the surface as it was sixty-five million years ago, they find a thin layer of this element spread everywhere.

The Gods

Some of the elements in the Periodic Table get their names from planets and asteroids, which were named after Roman gods. In the early nineteenth century, astronomers discovered two objects orbiting the Sun between Mars and Jupiter. They dubbed the first Ceres, after the goddess of harvest, and the second Pallas, for the Roman goddess of wisdom. The first element found after Ceres was named cerium, and the first element discovered after astronomers found Pallas was named palladium—the substance that Tony Stark uses to power his Iron Man exoskeleton in the movies.[*]

Palladium

Mercury, the silvery metal that's liquid and runny at

---

[*] Sorry, but this is pure fiction. The real palladium couldn't supply nearly endless stores of energy. Plutonium (see the next page) would be more feasible, but it's also highly radioactive, so Iron Man would become horribly ill or die before saving the world.

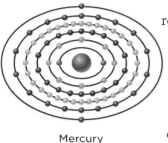

Mercury

room temperature, is named for the speedy Roman messenger god of the same name. Thorium is inspired by Thor, the hunky, lightning bolt–wielding Scandinavian god. No wonder Thor and Iron Man are such good friends. They share an elemental bond.

Saturn, my favorite planet,* has no element named for it, but Uranus, Neptune, and Pluto, all gods of Roman myths, are famously represented. Uranium was the main ingredient in the first atomic bomb ever used in warfare. Just as Neptune comes right after Uranus in the solar system, so too does neptunium come right after uranium in the Periodic Table.

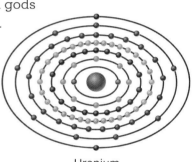

Uranium

The next element in the table, plutonium, is not found in nature. But scientists figured out how to make enough of it to pack into an atomic bomb, which the United States exploded over the Japanese city of Nagasaki, just three days after they dropped a uranium-fueled bomb on Hiroshima, bringing a swift end to World War II. Small quantities of certain kinds of plutonium could

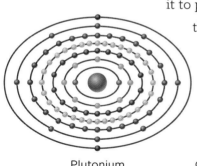

Plutonium

---

* Actually, Earth is my favorite planet. Then Saturn.

one day be used to fuel spacecraft that travel to the outer solar system.

So ends our cosmic journey through the Periodic Table of Chemical Elements, right to the edge of the solar system, and beyond. For reasons I have yet to understand, many people don't like chemicals. Perhaps the names just sound dangerous. But in that case we should blame the chemists, not the chemicals themselves. Personally, I am quite comfortable with chemicals. My favorite stars, as well as my best friends, are all made of them.

8.
Why the World
Is Round

The planet Saturn pops into my mind every time I
take a bite of a hamburger. There's nothing very
planetary about the food on its own. But the
shape of the burger, and the top bun especially,
is cosmic. It reminds me of how much the universe loves
the perfectly round balls known as spheres, and how these
circular objects change as they spin.

Saturn, for example. This jumbo planet spins around
much faster than Earth. Your day is twenty-four hours long
because it takes a given spot on our planet, such as where
you're sitting or standing right now, twenty-four hours
to complete one rotation. Earth carries anything on its
equator, which is the planet's waistline, at 1,000 miles per
hour. That probably sounds fast. An airliner only travels

at around 550 miles per hour. But neither of those speeds compares to Saturn. My second favorite planet completes a day, or one complete rotation, in just ten and a half hours. And Saturn is much, much larger than Earth, too. So to complete that turn in time, Saturn's equator revolves at 22,000 miles per hour.

If our planet spun that quickly, your school day would last about twenty minutes. But summer vacation would be shorter, too, and we wouldn't actually be here in the first place.

Objects that rotate quickly tend to flatten. Earth, for example, is not a perfect sphere. Our planet spins around an imaginary line extending from the North Pole to the South Pole. The distance from one pole to the other along this line is shorter than the distance from one side of the planet through to the other, when measured at the equator. In other words, Earth is slightly flatter at the poles.

Behold Saturn, my second favorite planet! A single day on Saturn lasts only ten and a half hours.

Why Santa Should Vacation in Ecuador

If Earth rotated just sixteen times faster, then centrifugal forces, the same ones that push riders out to the borders of a merry-go-round or keep water in a bucket as you swing it around in a circle, would make everything at the equator weightless. Even now, at Earth's current rotational speed, chubby Santa Claus would weigh about a pound less on the equator than he would at the North Pole, where centrifugal force has no effect. Everybody likes to feel better about themselves on vacation, so if you're looking for Santa in the off-season, I'd start there.

And I mean slightly: the difference is only about twenty-six miles.

The faster an object spins, the more it flattens. Which brings me back to hamburgers. Since Saturn spins at 22,000 miles per hour, the planet is a full ten percent flatter, pole to pole, than its middle. The difference is noticeable even through a small amateur telescope. Far from a perfect sphere, Saturn is more like a burger, with a wide center and a flattened bun on top.

The universe loves spheres. Apart from crystals and broken rocks, not much else in the cosmos naturally comes with sharp angles. While many objects have peculiar shapes, the list of round things is practically endless and ranges from simple soap bubbles to galaxies and beyond.

Trivia

Flattened spheres are called oblate spheroids. Earth is an oblate spheroid, and so is Saturn.

The physical laws that guide the universe favor spheres over other shapes. Surface tension, for example. This force pulls the materials in the surface of an object closer together. Consider a soap bubble. The bubble itself is made of soap and water. Inside, a pocket of air is trapped. The surface tension of the liquid that makes a soap bubble squeezes air in all directions. It will, within moments of being formed, trap the volume of air using the least possible surface area. This makes the strongest possible bubble because the soapy film will not have to be spread any thinner than is absolutely necessary. And the shape that has the smallest surface area for an enclosed volume is a perfect sphere.

In fact, billions of dollars could be saved annually on packaging materials if all shipping boxes and all packages of food in the supermarket were spheres. The contents of a super-jumbo box of Cheerios would fit easily into a spherical carton with just a four-and-a-half inch radius. But nobody wants to chase packaged food down the aisle after it rolls off the shelves.

On orbiting space stations, where everything is weightless because of the lack of gravity, you can gently squirt out precise amounts of molten—or liquid—metal, and the little beads just float in midair. Once they cool, they start to harden, and surface tension forms them into absolutely perfect spheres.

For large cosmic objects such as planets and stars, surface tension is less important. Energy and gravity work to turn these objects into spheres. Gravity does not only pull apples from trees or warp space. It tries to collapse matter in all directions, shrinking it into a smaller and smaller space.

But gravity does not always win—the chemical bonds of solid objects are strong. The Himalayas, the world's largest mountain range, grew against the force of Earth's gravity because of the powerful rocks in our planet's crust.

Before you get excited about Earth's mighty mountains, you should know that compared with other planets, Earth has a fairly flat surface. To teeny humans hiking the Himalayas, our mountains seem giant. To a city kid like myself, a large hill can seem enormous. You would think that when viewed from a distance, Earth would look bumpy due to all the great mountains. But Earth, as a cosmic object, is remarkably smooth. If you had a super-duper, jumbo-gigantic finger, and you dragged it across Earth's surface (oceans and all), Earth would feel as smooth as a cue ball from a game of pool. Globes that show raised portions of Earth's mountain ranges are total exaggerations of reality.

The Himalayas, Earth's largest mountain range, couldn't grow any taller. Gravity would pull them down.

Sure, we have towering peaks and low valleys, but when viewed from space, our planet looks like a perfectly flat sphere.

In spite of Earth's mountains and valleys, as well as being flattened slightly from pole to pole, when viewed from space, Earth looks like a perfect sphere.

Earth's mountains are also puny when compared with some other mountains in the solar system. The largest on Mars, Olympus Mons, is 65,000 feet tall and nearly 300 miles wide at its base. It makes Alaska's Mount McKinley look like a molehill. Even Mount Everest is less than half as tall.

Unfair, you say? How could the Martians be so lucky? The cosmic mountain-building recipe is simple: the weaker the gravity on the surface of an object, the higher its mountains can reach. Mount Everest is about as tall as a mountain on Earth can grow before the lower rock layers crumble under its weight. Any higher and gravity would pull it down.

Mars, on the other hand, has much lower gravity than Earth. A 70-pound fourth grader would weigh only 26 pounds on Mars. Because there is less gravity, the mountains can grow taller, which is why Olympus Mons towers so high.

The stars that decorate a clear night sky are round, too. They're big, massive blobs of gas, formed into near-perfect spheres thanks to gravity. But if a star gets too close to another object whose gravity is strong, the other object starts to strip away some of its material. This is common with binary stars, the pairs that are bound to each other by gravity, especially when one of them is an enormous dying star called a red giant. The other star in the pair starts

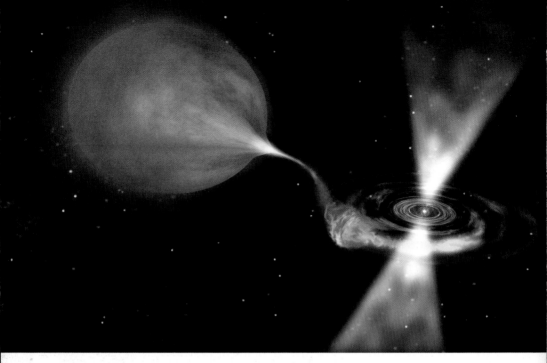

The spinning neutron star in this artist's version of a binary system sucks material from its dying neighbor, a glowing red giant.

sucking material from the red giant, distorting it into a shape that resembles a stretched-out Hershey's kiss.

Now we're going to get weird.

Imagine stuffing about a hundred million elephants into a tube of ChapStick.

To reach this density, you must do some intense work. Inside atoms, protons and neutrons are packed into the center while the electrons orbit the outside. Between those orbiting electrons and the tightly packed center of atoms, there's empty space. To squeeze all those elephants into a container of lip balm, you must compress all the empty space between the electrons and the center of atoms. Doing so will crush nearly all (negatively charged) electrons into (positively charged) protons, creating a ball of (neutrally charged) neutrons.

Meet the pulsar, another of my favorite cosmic objects. It is made from gas clouds, not elephants, but it is just as

This neutron star, a pulsar named Vela, spins faster than the blades of a helicopter.

dense as our pachyderms-in-the-tube example, and has crazy-high surface gravity. A mountain on a pulsar might grow no taller than the thickness of this page. But because of gravity, it would take you more energy to climb that tiny hill than a rock climber on Earth would need to scale a three-thousand-mile-high cliff.

We expect pulsars to be the most perfectly shaped spheres in the universe.

Galaxies are organized into clusters, and the shape of these clusters varies. Some are raggedy. Others are stretched thin in threads. Yet others form vast sheets. But the beautiful Coma cluster of galaxies, which we met in our chapter on dark matter, forms a beautiful sphere.

The Coma cluster is also what we call a "relaxed" system. Please resist the image of a group of galaxies kicking back and listening to smooth jazz. The "relaxing" I'm referring to here is of a different kind. It means many things, including the fact that you can guess the mass of the system by studying the speed and direction of the galaxies moving around within it. You don't have to see every massive object, however. By tracking those galaxies, scientists can also guess how much unseen or "dark" matter is hiding in the system, changing how those galaxies move.

It's for these reasons that relaxed systems make excellent probes of dark matter. Allow me to make an even stronger statement: were it not for relaxed systems, we might not have figured out that dark matter is everywhere in the cosmos.

The largest and most perfect sphere of all is the observable universe, or that part of the cosmos we can see with our telescopes.

In every direction we look, galaxies are racing away from us. The farther away the galaxy, the faster it's moving. There is a distance in every direction from us where objects are moving away from us as fast as the speed of light. At this distance and beyond, light that shines from objects such as stars loses all its energy before reaching us. Crossing the expanding cosmos, the light becomes stretched out and dulled. And if the light from such objects cannot reach us, then these objects are no longer observable. Since these limits extend in all directions, they form a sphere.

The universe beyond this spherical "edge" is invisible to us and, as far as we know, unknowable. But that shouldn't stop you from wondering what might lie out there in the great beyond.

9.
The Invisible Universe

On November 11, 1572, the Danish astronomer Tycho Brahe was out for an evening stroll when he noticed a spectacular new object in the sky. Brahe, who once had part of his nose sliced off in a duel, did not use telescopes to study the stars. Neither did the other astronomers of his day. Yet Brahe had been watching the heavens long enough to know that this object was a newcomer to the night sky.

What Brahe spotted that night was an exploding star known as a supernova.

Most supernovas appear in distant galaxies, but when a star blows up within our own Milky Way galaxy, it is bright enough for everyone to see, even without a telescope. Indeed, the wondrous visible light of that 1572 explosion was widely reported. Another supernova

Tycho's Nose

The famed astronomer Tycho Brahe didn't lose his nose in just any old duel. Apparently the fight sprang from an argument about math. He also lived in a castle and kept an elk as a pet. As for the fake nose he wore for most of his life, it was rumored to be made of silver or gold, but scientists actually dug up the famous scientist's remains a few years ago, and they found traces of brass around the bones of his nose. There are also rumors—still unconfirmed—that he may have been murdered. I assure you, friends, that the life of a modern astrophysicist is not nearly as dramatic.

event, in 1604, caused a similar sensation. Unfortunately, these were the last two supernova spectaculars hosted by our galaxy.

Today we rely on powerful telescopes to study exploding stars in distant reaches of the universe. Every bit of information a telescope delivers to the astrophysicist comes to Earth on a beam of light. But supernovas don't just release visible light, the kind that's convenient for the human eye. Some of the light they send our way is, to our eyes, invisible.

Our modern telescopes can catch all types of light, and

without them, astrophysicists would be totally unaware of some mind-blowing stuff in the universe.

Before 1800 the word "light," apart from its use a verb and an adjective, referred just to visible light. But early that year the English astronomer William Herschel, already well known for discovering the planet Uranus[*] in 1781, was exploring the relation between sunlight, color, and heat. Herschel began by placing a prism, a glass instrument that separates light into its different colors, in the path of a sunbeam. Nothing new there. Sir Isaac Newton had done that back in the 1600s, leading Newton to name the familiar seven colors of the rainbow: red, orange, yellow, green, blue, indigo, and violet.

Newton had used the prism to separate a sunbeam into its colors, but Herschel was curious enough to wonder if the temperature of each color might be different. So he placed thermometers in various regions of the rainbow. Sure enough, he showed that different colors registered different temperatures. The red light was warmer than the violet, for example.

Yet he also laid a thermometer outside the colors, beyond the red light. He guessed it would read no more than room temperature. But that's not what happened. The temperature of this thermometer rose even higher than the one placed in the red. That meant the sunbeam was hid-

* Stop laughing. Really.

Roy G. Biv

An easy trick to remember the order of the colors is to take the first letter of each, which combined spell out the name Roy G. Biv. Of course, Mr. Biv is an imaginary character, but I suspect he would have an impressive moustache, and maybe use a walking stick.

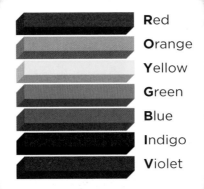

Red
Orange
Yellow
Green
Blue
Indigo
Violet

ing some new type of light, in addition to the colors he'd been studying.

An invisible beam of light.

Herschel had accidentally discovered "infra" red light, a brand-new part of what we call the electromagnetic spectrum—a larger version of the rainbow that includes both visible and invisible light. Other investigators immediately took up where Herschel left off. In 1801 a German physicist found proof of invisible light next to the violet end of the spectrum. What's beyond violet? "Ultra" violet, better known today as UV.

Filling out the rest of the spectrum, in order of low energy and low frequency to high energy and high frequency, we have radio waves, microwaves, infrared, Roy G. Biv, ultraviolet, X-rays, and gamma rays. While many of these forms of light were new or unfamiliar to the scientists of old, today we have learned to use and study all of them.

Mysteriously, astrophysicists were a bit slow to build telescopes that could see all these forms of invisible light. For more than three centuries, scientists thought of a telescope as a way to strengthen our limited eyesight, like a pair of cosmic spectacles. The bigger the telescope, the more distant the objects it brings into view; the more perfectly shaped its mirrors, the sharper the image it makes. But these new forms of light required new hardware. Detecting X-rays, for example, requires super-smooth mirrors. If you're gathering long radio waves, your detector doesn't need to be that precise, but it should be as big as you can afford to make it.

Supernovas send out all kinds of visible and invisible light, but no single combination of telescope and detector can see all of them at the same time. The way around that problem is simple: gather pictures from multiple telescopes and stitch them all together. Although we can't "see" invisible light, we can assign certain colors to different types of light, and create a single image that combines the findings of all the different telescopes and detectors.

This is precisely what I did for my friend Superman. In the comic, that is. When he visits me and my associates at the Hayden Planetarium, I explain that we hadn't just gathered information from our telescopes. To observe the death of his home planet's sun, we asked observatories across the world to point toward Superman's home. Gathering all the information collected by so many telescopes and detectors and pasting them into a single, visible image is an enormous challenge. In the story, in fact, this job was too much for the planetarium's computers. So Superman himself—whose mind is apparently a supercomputer—stitches them together to reveal a picture of his sun exploding in visible, infrared, and other forms of light.

I know people are into the whole bulletproof, laser eyes, flight thing. But processing that much astrophysical data faster than a supercomputer?

That is *real* power.

The earliest telescopes built to look for invisible light were radio telescopes. They are an amazing type of observatory. The American engineer Karl G. Jansky built the first successful one between 1929 and 1930. It looked a bit like the moving sprinkler system on a farmerless farm. Made from a series of tall, rectangular metal frames, it turned in place like a merry-go-round, but on wheels built with spare parts from a Model T Ford, a popular car from a few years earlier. Jansky had set up the hundred-foot-

Karl Jansky's telescope was compared to a merry-go-round because it rotated as it captured radio waves from the cosmos.

long contraption to capture a wavelength of about fifteen meters.

At the time, scientists believed radio waves came only from local thunderstorms or other sources on Earth. Using his strange antenna, Jansky discovered that radio waves can also be traced to the center of the Milky Way galaxy. With that observation, radio astronomy was born.

Scientists were finally watching the sky for more than visible light.

Modern radio telescopes are sometimes downright humongous. MK 1, which began its working life in 1957, is the planet's first genuinely gigantic radio telescope—

The 250-foot-wide MK 1 telescope, located in England, began searching for radio waves in 1957.

a single, steerable, 250-foot-wide, solid-steel dish at the Jodrell Bank Observatory near Manchester, England. The world's largest radio telescope, completed in 2016, is called the Five-hundred-meter Aperture Spherical radio Telescope, or "FAST" for short. At a cost of one hundred and eighty million dollars, it was built by China in Guizhou Province, and is larger in area than thirty football fields.

If aliens ever give us a call, the Chinese will be the first to know.

Searching for microwaves, we've got the sixty-six antennas of ALMA, the Atacama Large Millimeter Array, in the remote Andes Mountains of northern Chile, in South America. ALMA allows astrophysicists to follow cosmic action that can't be seen with other telescopes. We can watch giant gas clouds transform into the nurseries from which stars are born.

ALMA is located, by intention, in the most arid landscape on Earth—three miles above sea level and well above the wettest clouds. The water vapor in Earth's atmosphere chews up the microwave signals that ALMA and other

In the remote Andes Mountains, the sixty-six antennas of ALMA act as one giant telescope, allowing scientists to study how stars are born.

detectors try to catch. Astrophysicists want these signals to reach our telescopes with as little interference as possible. So if you want clean observations of cosmic objects, you must minimize the amount of water vapor between your telescope and the universe, just as ALMA has done.

Generally, dry skies far from major cities are a good place to observe the universe. It's the main reason my favorite summer vacation destination as a kid, Camp Uraniborg, was based in the desert.

We've covered long radio waves and microwaves. At the ultrashort-wavelength end of the spectrum you find the high-frequency, high-energy gamma rays. Discovered in 1900, they were not detected from space until a new kind of telescope was placed aboard NASA's *Explorer XI* satellite in 1961.

Anybody who reads too many comic books knows that gamma rays are bad for you. A gamma ray experiment gone wrong is the supposed reason that scientist Bruce Banner transforms into the green, muscular, rage-filled Hulk of the *Avengers* movies. But gamma rays are also hard to trap. They pass right through ordinary lenses and mirrors. So instead of catching them directly, the guts of *Explorer XI*'s telescope included a device that captured evidence of gamma rays as they raced through.

Two years later, the United States launched a new series of satellites, the *Velas*, to scan for bursts of gamma rays.

My Least Favorite Superhero

No, gamma rays will not transform you into a giant green monster. But that's not what bothers me about the Hulk, scientifically. When Bruce Banner, a man of average size, turns into the Hulk, he becomes nine feet tall and weighs hundreds of pounds. Maybe more. Banner *gains* mass—a violation of the laws of physics. You can't just conjure mass out of thin air. I suppose he could be transforming energy into all this new matter in his body, but if he did that, then he might knock out all the power in the surrounding city.

The United States was worried that the Soviet Union was testing dangerous new nuclear weapons. Such tests would release gamma rays, so the United States dispatched the satellites to search for evidence. The *Velas* indeed found bursts of gamma rays, almost daily. But Russia wasn't to blame. The gamma ray signals were coming from explosions across the universe.

Today, telescopes search for light in every invisible part of the spectrum. We can now observe low-frequency radio waves a dozen meters long, crest to crest. We can study high-frequency gamma rays no longer than a quadrillionth of a meter—an unimaginably small distance from the peak of one wave to the next.

For the astrophysicist, these telescopes are tools for answering all kinds of questions. Curious how much gas lurks among the stars in galaxies? Radio telescopes can tell you. Interested in the cosmic background and the big bang? Microwave telescopes are critical. Want to peek deep inside galactic gas clouds, to study how stars are born? Infrared telescopes will help. How about examining black holes? Ultraviolet and X-ray telescopes are best. Want to watch the high-energy explosion of a giant star? Catch the drama via gamma ray telescopes.

In the days of Tycho Brahe, there were so many discoveries yet to be made. But I much prefer being a skywatcher today, and not only because this is a slightly more civilized time, and no one has attempted to chop off my nose. This is an amazing time to be an astrophysicist because we know that some of the most exciting action in the universe is invisible.

And we can see all of it.*

---

* Except for dark matter. But we're getting there.

10.
Around Our Solar Neighborhood

An alien staring back at our solar system might conclude it looks empty. The Sun, all planets, and their moons occupy a tiny fraction of the solar system. But our solar system isn't empty. Not even close. The space between the planets contains all manner of chunky rocks, pebbles, ice balls, dust, streams of charged particles, and far-flung probes.

Our solar system is so not-empty that Earth, as it races through its orbit, plows through hundreds of tons of meteors per day—most of them no larger than a grain of sand. Nearly all of them burn in Earth's upper atmosphere, the layer of air that surrounds our planet. These meteors slam into the atmosphere with so much energy that they vaporize on contact. That is a good thing. Without this protective blanket of air, our ancestors might have been destroyed by space rocks long before we could evolve into our current Instagram-posting selves.

Larger, golf-ball-size meteors often shatter into many smaller pieces before they vaporize. Still larger meteors are singed on their surface as they crash through the atmosphere, but otherwise make it all the way to the ground intact. Early in our planet's history, so much junk rained

Voyager 1 and Voyager 2

Launched in 1977, these spacecraft have been racing through space ever since. In 2012, *Voyager 2* became the first human-made craft to leave the solar system. *Voyager 1*, seen here, isn't far behind. You can track their progress here: https:// voyager.jpl.nasa.gov/mission/ status/.

down that the energy from the impacts melted our crust, the planet's hard outer layer.

One substantial hunk of space junk led to the formation of the Moon. The evidence indicates that an object the size of Mars careened off our young planet. The glancing collision sent chunks of dust and rock into orbit around Earth. This debris gradually bunched together into our lovely, low-density Moon.

Earth was not the only object bombarded by space rocks. The many craters on the surfaces of the Moon and Mercury are evidence of past crashes. Space is filled with rocks of all sizes that were ejected from the surface of Mars, the Moon, and Earth when high-speed objects struck the surface. About a thousand tons of Martian rocks rain down on Earth each year. Perhaps the same amount reaches Earth

Cashing In on Space Rocks

Most meteorites splash down into the oceans because water covers 72 percent of our planet's surface. But collecting meteorites is a passionate and sometimes expensive habit. One meteorite hunter once called them "money from the sky," and the right space rock certainly can earn you some cash. In 2012, someone sold a chunk of rock from the Moon for $330,000.

from the Moon. So maybe we didn't have to send astronauts to the Moon to retrieve Moon rocks. Plenty come to us.

Most of the solar system's asteroids live in the main asteroid belt, a roughly flat zone between the orbits of Mars and Jupiter. Shaped more like a flattened donut than an actual belt, this area is often drawn as a region of cluttered, meandering rocks. Any one of a group of these asteroids, perhaps a few thousand, could one day crash into Earth. Most will hit our planet within a hundred million years. The ones larger than about a kilometer across will collide with enough energy to put most of Earth's land species at risk of extinction.

That would be bad.

Comets also pose a risk to life on Earth. The most famous of them all, Halley's comet, can be seen streaking through the night sky roughly every 75 years. This giant hunk of ice and rock is older than Earth itself and last appeared in 1986. If it were to strike our planet, it would do so with the force of ten million volcanic eruptions.

That would be bad, too.

But Halley won't be back again until 2061, and it won't pass close enough to end civilization. If you're around then, and not too busy preparing for your trip to a Moon hotel or repairing your household robot, I suggest you find a decent telescope.

Halley's comet, pictured here, is a joy to observe, but we don't want it traveling too close to our surface. That would be bad.

Far beyond the Kuiper belt, extending halfway to the nearest stars, lives a group of comets called the Oort cloud. This zone is responsible for long-period comets, those with orbits so large that it takes far longer than a human lifetime for them to complete one trip. The two brightest of the 1990s, comets Hale-Bopp and Hyakutake, were both from the Oort cloud. They're not coming back anytime soon, so you missed your chance. But I can assure you, they were stunning. Hyakutake was so bright that it could even be seen (without a telescope) from the middle of Times Square in New York City.

Last I had kept count, there were fifty-six moons among the planets in the solar system. Then I woke up one morning to learn that another dozen had been discovered around Saturn. After that, I decided to no longer keep track. All I care about now is whether any of them would be fun places to visit or study. And I can think of at least a few candidates. By some measures, the solar system's moons are much more fascinating than the planets they orbit.

On Titan, the largest moon of my second favorite planet, tributaries flow into rivers, which run into giant lakes. The liquid in these lakes is methane, not water, and we have sent a spacecraft to study this moon. But a closer look would no doubt reveal more fascinating details.

My favorite moons might be the ones orbiting the planet Jupiter. This system is filled with oddballs. Io, Jupiter's closest moon, is the most volcanically active place in the solar system, and far too hot to visit. Another of Jupiter's moons, Europa, is covered with ice, so it wouldn't be an ideal vacation spot, either. But in terms of our quest for extraterrestrial life, it's one of the most exciting places in the solar system. If ever there was a next-best place to look for life, it's here.

At first glance, astrophysicists might not pick Europa as a good spot for life. Typically, we look for planets and moons in the Goldilocks zone, which we discussed in chapter 1. The young blond trespasser didn't like her porridge too hot or too cold, and astrophysicists feel the same way

Mission to Europa

We all want to go to Europa. Period. The potential science discoveries are phenomenal. But we would have to tackle some amazing engineering challenges. First we'd have to send a spacecraft to the moon. Then this craft, or a smaller one that fits inside, would have to descend from orbit to Europa's frozen surface. Then we'd have to go ice fishing. The sheet of ice that covers the ocean is probably more than a mile thick, and we would have to tunnel or drill through to the water beneath. Next, the mission would require another probe or submarine capable of swimming around in that water, collecting information, and sending it back to us eager scientists here on Earth. A major challenge, yes. But imagine what we might find.

about planets capable of supporting life. We look for areas that aren't too close to the nearest star, as that would vaporize any water on the surface, and we know that liquid water is essential to life. But venture too far from the host star—in Europa's case, the Sun—and the water would freeze. The spot would be too cold. What we try to find are planets in that not-too-hot, not-too-cold category.

Europa lies outside the Goldilocks zone, and its frozen surface doesn't look like a place for life to thrive. But it turns out Europa doesn't need the Sun. As the moon orbits Jupiter, its shape changes. The gravitational pull of the planet squeezes and releases the moon as it whips around. This process of squeezing and releasing the moon actually pumps energy into Europa, warming the water beneath the icy surface of the ocean. There's no reason to think this warm water hasn't been there for billions of years. If we want to find life somewhere other than our planet, Europa should be our next destination.

By tradition, planets are named for Roman gods, and their moons for personalities from Greek mythology. The classical gods led complicated social lives, so there is no shortage of characters. The lone exception to this rule applies to the moons of Uranus, which are named for assorted heroes from British plays and poems. Instead of Europa and Io, you'll find Puck and Ariel, both fairies in the plays of William Shakespeare. (Not a rubber disc you slap with a hockey stick or a little mermaid.)

In 1781, William Herschel, the scientist who discovered invisible light, also became the first person to find a planet beyond those we can see with our eyes. He was ready to name it after the king, under whom he faithfully served. Had Herschel succeeded, the planet list would read: Mercury, Venus, Earth, Mars, Jupiter, Saturn, and George. Fortunately, the classical name Uranus, god of the sky, was adopted some years later.

Although all the planets and moons in our solar system have already been named, there are plenty of asteroids left to be tagged. The discoverers get to name them whatever they like, and I am now responsible for some of the solar system's space junk. In November 2000, the main-belt asteroid 1994KA, discovered by David Levy and Carolyn Shoemaker, was named 13123 Tyson in my honor. While I was appreciative, there's no particular reason to get big-headed about it; plenty of asteroids have familiar names such as Jody, Harriet, and Thomas. There are even asteroids out there named Merlin, James Bond, and Santa. Now in the hundreds of thousands, the asteroid count might soon challenge our ability to name them. Whether or not that day arrives, I'm happy knowing that my chunk of cosmic debris is not alone as it litters the space among the planets.

I'm also glad that, at the moment, my asteroid is not headed toward Earth.

11.
What Earth Would Look Like to an Alien

To understand how Earth would appear to a distant, intelligent group of aliens, let's take a look at our planet from the ground up, and out.

Whether you prefer to sprint, swim, walk, or ride your bike from one place to another on Earth, you can enjoy close-up views of our planet's unlimited supply of things to notice. You might see a spider trapping a moth in its web, a drop of water flowing off a leaf, a hermit crab scurrying along the sand, or a pimple on a teenager's nose.

On the ground, Earth is rich in detail. All you have to do is look.

Now move up and away. From the window of a rising airplane, those surface details rapidly disappear. No spider appetizers. No frightened crabs. No pimples. Reach cruising altitude, around seven miles up, and identifying your town becomes a challenge.

Detail continues to vanish as you rise into space. The International Space Station orbits at about 250 miles up. Through one of its windows, you might find Paris, London, New York, and Los Angeles in the daytime, but only if you know your geography. You probably won't even see the Great Pyramids at Giza, and you certainly won't see the Great Wall of China.

If you're standing on the Moon, a quarter million miles away, New York, Paris, and the rest of Earth's glittering cities won't even show up as a twinkle. But you can still watch masses of cold air and other major weather fronts sweep across the planet. Let's say you move to Mars when it's closest to Earth, some thirty-five million miles away. Giant snow-capped mountain chains and the edges of Earth's continents would be visible through a large

Trivia

Can you see the Great Wall of China from space? No! Although the Great Wall is thousands of miles long, it's only about twenty feet wide—much narrower than the U.S. highways you can barely see from a high-flying airplane.

Captured by the *Voyager 1* space probe, this image was the first to include Earth and the Moon in a single frame. Once the spacecraft traveled beyond Neptune's orbit, Earth was just a "pale blue dot" in the distance.

backyard telescope. But that would be all. You wouldn't be able to see that we have cities.

Travel out to Neptune, three billion miles away, and the Sun itself becomes a thousand times dimmer, compared with our view from Earth. And what of Earth? It's a speck no brighter than a dim star, all but lost in the glare of the Sun.

We have proof: In 1990, the *Voyager 1* spacecraft took a photograph of Earth from just beyond Neptune's orbit. Our planet looks underwhelming from deep space: a "pale blue dot," as the American astrophysicist Carl Sagan called it. And that's generous. If you were to glance at the *Voyager 1* photo, you might not even know Earth is there.

What would happen if some big-brained aliens from the great beyond scanned the skies with state-of-the-art telescopes? What visible features of planet Earth might they detect?

Blueness. That would be first and foremost. Water covers more than two-thirds of Earth's surface; the Pacific Ocean alone spans nearly an entire side of the planet. If these aliens were able to detect our planet's color, they would probably guess that the source of all this blue was water. They'd most likely be familiar with water, too. Not only does water appear to support life. It's one of the most abundant molecules in the universe.

If the aliens had really powerful equipment, they would see more than just a pale blue dot. They would see coastlines, too, strongly suggesting that the water is liquid, since a frozen planet would not have coasts. And smart aliens would surely know that if a planet has liquid water, then it might host life.

The aliens could also see Earth's polar ice caps, which grow and shrink as the temperature changes. By studying the surface, and tracking how often the major landmasses rotate out of and back into view, they would also be able to figure out that our planet rotates every twenty-four hours. They'd

The nearest planet in orbit around a star other than the Sun hides here in Alpha Centauri, a system four light-years away.

Alpha Centauri AB

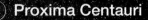 Proxima Centauri

know the length of our days. The aliens would see major weather systems come and go. They could study our clouds.

Time for a reality check.

The nearest exoplanet—the nearest planet in orbit around a star that is not the Sun—can be found in our neighbor star system Alpha Centauri. That's about four light-years away, or the distance covered by a beam of light speeding for four straight years, without stopping for fuel or a bathroom break. Light travels more than six hundred and seventy million miles in a single hour. So our "neighbors" in Alpha Centauri, at a four-light-year distance, are far, far away.

Those are the close ones. Most of the exoplanets scientists have discovered lie from dozens up to hundreds of light-years away. Earth is less than one-billionth as bright as the Sun, so it would be extremely hard for any of those aliens to see our planet directly with a visible light telescope. It's like trying to detect the light of a firefly near a giant searchlight. So if aliens have found us, they are likely looking at our invisible light, like infrared. The Sun doesn't outshine us quite as much in the infrared.

Or maybe their engineers are adopting a totally different strategy altogether.

I imagine you've photobombed a friend's picture before. Even accomplished astrophysicists can't resist the lure of this common prank, and photobombing also has some sim-

The amazing Kepler spacecraft allowed scientists to discover thousands of new planets. Does one of them harbor life?

ilarities to one of the tricks we use to find distant planets. Just as aliens might struggle to see Earth from a distance, it's hard for us to see faraway planets directly. So NASA designed and built a telescope, Kepler, that searched for tiny planets as they photobombed nearby stars.

The Kepler telescope watched stars whose total brightness drops slightly, and on a regular basis. In these cases, Kepler's line of sight was just right to see a star get dimmer, by a tiny fraction, due to one of its own planets crossing directly in front of the host star, like a gnat flying through a picture of you and your friends. With this method, you can't see the planet itself. You can't even see any features on the star's surface. But you can see that something is there. Kepler discovered thousands of exoplanets, including hundreds of star systems with multiple planets like our own.

Aliens could use the same technique to identify Earth. By watching the Sun, they would be able to detect a slight drop in brightness when our planet passed between them and our local star. Fine. They'd discover Earth exists, but they would learn nothing about the happenings on our surface.

Radio waves and microwaves might help. Maybe our eavesdropping aliens would have something like FAST, the enormous 500-meter radio telescope in China that we discussed in chapter 9. If they did, and if they tuned to the right frequencies, we would appear to be one of the brightest sources in the sky. Our modern radios, mobile phones, microwave ovens, garage-door openers, car-door unlockers, and communications satellites are all cranking out signals. We're ablaze in these long waves. If the aliens were using the right telescopes and detectors, this would be spectacular evidence that something unusual was going on here.

Earth would look like a pretty interesting party.

Mysterious radio signals once stumped our own scientists, leading them to wonder, briefly, if aliens were trying to communicate with us. In 1967, while searching the skies for any source of strong radio waves, astrophysicist Antony Hewish and his team discovered something extremely odd. A faraway object was pulsing slightly more than once per second. Jocelyn Bell, a graduate student of Hewish's at the time, was the first to notice it.

The thought that the signal came from another culture beaming evidence of its activities across space—an alien, radio-based version of, "Hey, over here!"—was irresistible.

who Gets the Prize?

Although scientists do credit Jocelyn Bell—now Jocelyn Bell Burnell—with the discovery of pulsars, the Nobel Prize for the work was awarded to her boss, Antony Hewish. In 1977, Bell Burnell insisted that she was not upset about the snub, but many others have said she would have won as well if not for her gender. Her contribution to the discovery of pulsars and ongoing work have earned Bell Burnell many other awards since, and she has been a tremendous advocate for women in science.

But Bell herself found it frustrating. She was trying to earn her graduate degree at the time, and these little green men and their signal were interfering. Within a few days, however, she discovered other repeating signals coming from other places in our Milky Way galaxy. Bell and the other scientists realized they hadn't made contact with aliens, but they had discovered a new class of cosmic object—a star made entirely of neutrons that pulses with radio waves with every rotation. (And the same one that's as dense as a ChapStick casing with a hundred million elephants packed inside.) Hewish and Bell sensibly called them "pulsars." And Bell didn't just earn her graduate degree. She was credited with one of the most important discoveries of the twentieth century.

There are other ways to snoop on aliens—or for advanced extraterrestrials to snoop on us. Extraterrestrials could study the light from our planet to see what kind of molecules exist on and around Earth. If a planet is teeming with plant and animal life, its atmosphere will be rich with what we call biomarkers. Not to be confused with magic markers, these molecules are more like clues. When a planet has biomarkers, scientists know that life could be present. These molecules thrive when life is around.

On Earth, methane is one such biomarker. Natural sources such as rotting vegetation contribute some of our methane. The rest is produced by human-related activities such as fuel oil production, rice cultivation, sewage, and the burps and farts of domestic livestock.

Yes, cow farts could one day help aliens discover us.

The most telling sign for our aliens, though, would be all the free-floating oxygen in our atmosphere. Oxygen is the third most common element in the cosmos. It's also chemically active, the atomic version of the kid at the middle school dance who will get down with just about anyone on the floor. Oxygen bonds with atoms of hydrogen, carbon, nitrogen, silicon, and so on. It even bonds with itself. This molecule doesn't like to be alone and free.

So, if aliens saw oxygen in a free-floating state, they might guess that something is setting it loose. Here on Earth, we know that life is responsible. Photosynthesis, the

Are There Cows on Titan?

Scientists are currently arguing about the origin of the small amounts of methane on Mars and the abundant quantities on Saturn's moon Titan. Where did it all come from? Not cosmic cows, unfortunately. Titan has rivers flowing with methane. Entire lakes are filled with this biomarker.

process that plants use to transform the Sun's light into fuel, creates free oxygen in the oceans and in the atmosphere. That free oxygen in the air allows humans and practically every other creature in the animal kingdom to survive.

We Earthlings already know why oxygen and other biomarkers are important. But these aliens would have to figure all that out for themselves. If they decided that these clues are sure evidence of life, maybe they'd even wonder if the life is intelligent. Sometimes I ask that question myself.

But, really—are aliens out there, searching the cosmos for signs of life? The first exoplanet was discovered in 1995, and as of this writing, the tally is rising through four thousand. Scientists now think as many as forty billion Earth-sized planets exist in the Milky Way alone. With numbers like that, somewhere out there, someone or something might be watching.

12.
Looking Up, Thinking Big

As a kid, one of the hardest truths to learn is that you're not actually the center of the universe. I remember my fifth birthday. My mother came home from the store and stuck a candle in the middle of the cake. The candle was in the shape of the number five. I was *amazed*. The people at the store knew that I was turning five! They made and kept that candle just for me.

That's what I thought, anyway. It never occurred to me that other children, all over the world, had turned or would soon turn five, and that there were many of these candles. So what does this have to do with stars and galaxies?

Astrophysics teaches us that we're not the center of the world.

It teaches us that our universe might not even be the only universe. It teaches us to have a cosmic perspective.

But who gets to think that way? Who gets to celebrate this cosmic view of life? Not the farmworkers who have to move from job to job just to feed their families. Not the factory worker building electronics for little pay. Certainly not the homeless person rummaging through the trash for food. You need the luxury of time not spent on mere survival. Or you need to be young, comfortable enough that you don't need to worry about food or safety, and willing to look up from your apps or texts or latest series on Netflix, and out at the stars.

The cosmic view comes with a hidden cost. When I travel thousands of miles to spend a few moments in the fast-moving shadow of the Moon during a total solar eclipse, sometimes I lose sight of Earth.

When I pause and reflect on our expanding universe, with its galaxies hurtling away from one another, embedded within the ever-stretching fabric of space and time, sometimes I forget that uncounted people walk this Earth without food or shelter, and that many of them are children like you.

When I track the orbits of asteroids, comets, and planets, each one a pirouetting dancer in a cosmic ballet, guided by gravity, sometimes I forget that too many people ignore the delicate relationship between Earth's atmosphere, oceans, and land.

And sometimes I forget that powerful people rarely do all they can to help those who cannot help themselves.

I occasionally forget those things because however big the world is—in our hearts, our minds, and our outsized digital maps—the universe is even bigger. A depressing thought to some, but a liberating thought to me.

I'm sure the adults in your life scold you occasionally, and announce that your problems *are not that important.* Maybe they even remind you that the world doesn't revolve around you. But we grown-ups need to tell ourselves that as well.

Now imagine a world in which everyone, but especially people with power and influence, holds an expanded view of our place in the cosmos. With that perspective, our problems would shrink—or never arise at all—and we could celebrate our small earthly differences, not fight and argue because of them.

Back in January 2000, the newly rebuilt Hayden Planetarium in New York City featured a space show titled *Passport to the Universe,* which took visitors on a virtual zoom from the planetarium out to the edge of the cosmos. The audience viewed Earth and then the solar system, and then watched the hundred billion stars of the Milky Way galaxy shrink, in turn, to barely visible dots on the planetarium's dome.

Within a month of opening day, I received a letter from a college professor whose expertise was in things that make people feel insignificant or small. I never knew one could specialize in such a field. He wanted to hand out a before-and-after questionnaire to visitors, to see how depressed they were after viewing the show. *Passport to the Universe*, he wrote, made him feel terrible.

How could that be? Every time I see the space show (and others we've produced), I feel alive and spirited and connected. I also feel large, knowing that the three-pound human brain is what enabled us to figure out our place in the universe.

Allow me to suggest that it's the professor, not I, who has misread nature. His ego was unjustifiably big to begin with, inflated by the idea that human beings are more important than everything else in the universe.

In all fairness to the fellow, powerful forces in society leave most of us thinking this way. I thought this way myself, until the day I learned in biology class that more of the microscopic bugs called bacteria live and work in one tiny spot in my body than the number of people who have existed in the world. That kind of information makes you think twice about who—or what—is actually in charge.

I know what you're thinking: we're smarter than bacteria.

No doubt about it, we're smarter than every other living creature that ever ran, crawled, or slithered on Earth. But how smart is that? We cook our food. We compose poetry and music. We create art and do science. We're good at math. Even if you're bad at math, you're probably much better at it than the smartest chimpanzee. A chimpanzee can't do long division.

But maybe, on the cosmic scale, we're not that smart. Imagine a life form whose brainpower is to ours as ours is to a chimpanzee's. To such a species, our highest mental achievements would be nothing. Their toddlers, instead of learning their ABCs on *Sesame Street*, would study college-level math. To these creatures, Einstein would be no smarter than little Timmy who just came home from alien preschool.

Our genes—the codes that guide a human baby as it grows and transforms into a full-grown adult—are not that much different from those of a chimpanzee. We are a little smarter, yes. But really we are one with the rest of nature, fitting neither above nor below, but within.

Want to know what you're really made of? Again, the cosmic perspective offers a bigger answer than you might expect. The chemical elements of the universe are forged in the fires of high-mass stars that end their lives in huge explosions, enriching their host galaxies with the chemicals needed for life. The result? The four most common, chemically active ingredients in the universe—hydrogen, oxygen, carbon, and nitrogen—are the four most common elements of life on Earth.

We do not simply live in this universe.

The universe lives within us.

That being said, we may not even be of this Earth. Scientists have uncovered information that is forcing them to rethink who we are and where we came from.

First, as we've already seen, when a large asteroid strikes a planet, the surrounding areas can recoil from the impact energy, catapulting rocks into space. In the same way, if you were to place a small toy on your bed, then jump down onto the mattress, the energy from your impact would force the toy to spring into the air. Asteroids can strike with so much energy that the rocks freed from a planet's surface can travel to—and land on—other planets. That's how we find rocks from the Moon and Mars right here on Earth.

Second, the tiny forms of life called microorganisms can survive wide ranges of temperature, pressure, and radiation encountered during space travel. If space rocks come from a planet with life, then microscopic life forms could safely stow away inside.

Third, recent evidence suggests that shortly after the formation of our solar system, Mars was wet, and perhaps fertile enough for life.

Together, these findings tell us it's possible that life began on Mars and traveled to Earth inside a rock. So all Earthlings might—just might—be descendants of Martians.

Again and again across the centuries, cosmic discoveries have hurt our self-image. We used to think Earth was unique. Then astronomers learned that ours is just another planet orbiting the Sun. Okay, but the Sun was still special, right? Not when we learned that the countless stars of the night sky are suns themselves.

Fine, but our galaxy, the Milky Way, surely had to be unique.

Not really. Not after we established that the countless fuzzy things we see in the sky are other galaxies, dotting the landscape of our known universe.

Today, it's easy to think our universe is all there is. Yet new theories require that we remain open to another possibility, the idea that ours is just one of many universes, that we are merely part of a much larger multiverse.

The cosmic perspective flows from knowledge about the universe. But it's about more than what you know. It's also about having the wisdom and insight to apply that knowledge to assessing our place in the universe. And its attributes are clear:

★ The cosmic perspective comes from the frontiers of science, yet it is not solely for the scientist. It belongs to everyone.

★ The cosmic perspective is humble.

★ The cosmic perspective is spiritual but not religious.

★ The cosmic perspective enables us to grasp, in the same thought, the large and the small, from a universe that began in a space far tinier than the period at the end of this sentence to one that is now many billions of light-years across.

★ The cosmic perspective opens our minds to extraordinary ideas but does not leave them so open that we lose our ability to reason, leaving us quick to believe anything we're told.

✨ The cosmic perspective opens our eyes to the universe, not as a force that cradles and cares for life, but as a cold, lonely, dangerous place that's quick to extinguish life with extreme emptiness and all manner of hazardous objects. This makes us understand the value and importance of all humans—even your annoying siblings or bullying classmates.

✨ The cosmic perspective shows Earth to be a pale blue dot orbiting through the vastness of space. But it's a precious dot, and for the moment, it's the only home we have—encouraging us to care for our rare and welcoming planet.

✨ The cosmic perspective finds beauty in the images of planets, moons, and stars but also celebrates gravity and the other universal laws that shape them.

✨ The cosmic perspective helps us to see beyond our circumstances, allowing us to realize that life is about more than money, popularity, clothes, sports, or even grades.

✨ The cosmic perspective reminds us that space exploration should not be a race in which countries compete against one another for the next great achievement, but a cosmic quest that joins all nations together in search of knowledge and experience.

☆彡 The cosmic perspective not only tells us that life in all forms is rare, and that we have more in common with all the other forms of life on Earth than we thought in the past, but that we will probably share similarities with any yet-to-be discovered life in the universe.

☆彡 The cosmic perspective shows us that the very atoms and particles that make up our bodies are spread across the universe itself, making us one and the same.

At least once a week, if not once a day, I hope you take a moment to wonder what cosmic truths lie undiscovered before us. These mysteries await the arrival of a clever thinker, an ingenious experiment, or an inventive space mission. We might further wonder how those discoveries may one day transform life on Earth.

During our brief stay on planet Earth, we owe ourselves and our descendants the opportunity to explore—in part because it's fun to do, whether we send astronauts to Mars or robots to Europa and beyond. But there's a far nobler reason. The day our knowledge of the cosmos ceases to expand, we risk falling back to the childish view that the universe revolves around us. That there is only one five-shaped birthday candle in the entire world. This would be the end of the human quest for knowledge and truth. So I encourage you to work to ensure that this does not happen. The very future of humanity may depend on our ability to embrace, rather than fear, the cosmic perspective.

GLOSSARY

Antimatter: Matter is anything that takes up space, including protons, electrons, and the other basic particles. Each of these particles also has an antimatter twin that is its opposite in every way. Antimatter rarely survives long, however. When a proton meets its antimatter twin, the antiproton, they destroy each other, releasing a burst of energy.

Asteroids: These space rocks orbit the Sun and range in size from tiny pebbles to planetoids, or miniature planets, like Ceres, which measures almost 600 miles, or 1,000 kilometers, across. Tens of thousands of space rocks are collected in the main asteroid belt between Mars and Jupiter. One asteroid wiped out the dinosaurs.

Atom: Everything you see and touch and smell is made of atoms. They consist of a nucleus, or center, with at least one positively charged proton, and at least one electron in orbit around that center. Except for hydrogen, the simplest and

most common atom in the universe, all atoms have neutrons in their nucleus, too.

Big Bang: The birth of the universe, when all the matter
and energy that make up our galaxies and stars and planets and life forms rapidly burst outward from an unimaginably tiny space.

Comet: This solar system traveler, a favorite of amateur
and professional astronomers, is made of ice and dust.
The ice is a wonderful feature because it tends to melt as
a comet passes within range of the Sun, leaving behind a
visible trail of gas and dust.

Cosmic Microwave Background: Light left over from
the early days of the universe is still around today, shining across the cosmos. The universe has been expanding since the big bang, though, so this light has been
stretched out and transformed into longer, invisible light
called microwaves. Although we can't see these microwaves with our eyes, our telescopes can measure them
and give scientists clues about what was happening in the
early universe.

Cosmic Rays: These high-energy beams zip across the cosmos with tremendous power trapped inside a tiny package
of particles. Cosmic rays would be harmful to humans, but
our atmosphere provides a safety shield.

Cosmos: Another name for our vast, wonderful, and mysterious universe. It's also the title of a particularly stellar science TV series.

Dark Energy: The universe appears to be growing faster than it should be, according to what we know about gravity and the amount of matter in the cosmos. A mysterious force appears to be driving this growth. Scientists have named it dark energy.

Dark Matter: By studying distant galaxies and groups of galaxies, astrophysicists revealed that an unknown, invisible form of matter appears to be holding groups of stars together. Since we cannot see the stuff, scientists dubbed it dark matter. If you find out what it really is, please let me know.

Electromagnetic Force: One of the four main or fundamental forces in the universe, this force binds molecules together and holds electrons in orbit around the positively charged centers of atoms.

Electron: A particle with negative charge. As far as we know, you cannot break the electron up into smaller pieces, so we call it a fundamental particle.

Element: Atoms come in many different forms, depending on the number of protons packed into their nuclei, and the 118 elements that make up the Periodic Table of Chemical Elements describe all the known types of atoms in the universe.

Exoplanet: Any planet that orbits a star that is not the Sun is an exoplanet. The nearest one is four light-years away, or the distance covered by a beam of light speeding for four straight years. Scientists have discovered thousands of these faraway worlds in recent years. Could one of them support life? We're hoping to find out.

Galaxy: A group of stars, gas, dust, and dark matter bound by gravity.

Gravity: Another one of the four fundamental forces in the universe, gravity doesn't just keep your feet on the ground. Thanks to Einstein, we learned that it actually warps space, bending straight lines into curves.

Intergalactic Space: These dark stretches between galaxies, which appear empty at first glance, host exotic happenings such as runaway stars and superhot gases. See chapter 4, "Between the Galaxies."

Lepton: One of the first two particle types to appear in the universe, leptons are loners, and don't like clumping into groups. The best-known lepton is the electron.

Light-Year: Astrophysicists deal with very, very large distances, so kilometers or miles just aren't big enough for us. Instead, we use light-years, or the number of years it would take a beam of light, traveling at three hundred million meters per second, to travel from a distant object to our telescopes.

Matter: Anything that takes up space is considered matter, including you and everything around you—plus all the tiny quarks and leptons from which everything is built.

Neutron: A resident of the nucleus, or center of the atom, the neutron is made of quarks, but it has no charge. One of the most exotic objects in the universe, the neutron star, is packed with these particles.

Nucleus: The center of the atom, made up of protons and, except for hydrogen, neutrons.

Photon: A wave-like packet of light energy.

Proton: This positively charged member of the center of atoms is made up of quarks, and first appeared about one second after the birth of the universe. The simplest and most common element in the universe, hydrogen, has only one proton in its nucleus. Iron, one of the heavy elements, has twenty-six protons.

Pulsar: A neutron star (see "Neutron," above) that sends out beams of light as it spins, acting like a cosmic lighthouse.

Quark: This fundamental particle—in other words, you can't break it up into smaller pieces—comes in six different forms, and was one of the first types of matter to appear in the early universe, along with leptons. Without quarks, we wouldn't have protons or neutrons, or atoms . . . or much of anything at all.

Strong Force: Another one of the four fundamental forces, the strong force holds protons and neutrons together inside the nucleus. Although it is the strongest of the four forces, it only works over very short distances.

Weak Force: The fundamental force that controls radioactive decay, the process by which an atom breaks down and converts some of its matter into energy. The other three forces hold large and small forms of matter together, but the weak force slowly breaks it apart.

Wormhole: One of the stranger outcomes of Einstein's work on gravity, and his discovery that it warps space and time, is the idea that the universe could be bent back on itself, allowing for shortcuts from one place in the cosmos to another. No one has ever discovered one of these tunnels, known as wormholes, but many prominent scientists, including Einstein himself, have given serious thought to the concept. Wormholes are also a favorite tool of science fiction writers.

ILLUSTRATION CREDITS

INDEX

Note: *Italicized* page numbers refer to photos or illustrations.